UNDERSTANDING MOONSEED
ESSAYS OF LIFE

UNDERSTANDING MOONSEED
ESSAYS OF LIFE

MARY PACIFICO CURTIS

BLAZEVOX[BOOKS]
Buffalo, New York

publisher of weird little books

BlazeVOX [books]

blazevox.org

21 20 19 18 17 16 15 14 13 12 01 02 03 04 05 06 07 08 09 10 11

BlazeVOX

Acknowledgements

The following titles have been published as noted below.

Prick of the Spindle: *Chakras*

Prompt: *A Life In Architecture*

Streetlight: *JFK and Me*

Medium: *Flight to the Future*

Lost Magazine: *Honeymoons*
(2019 Finalist, New Millennium Award for Non-Fiction)

Six Hens: *Understanding Moonseed*

Crab Orchard Review: *Going Back*

Streetlight: *The Paradox Formation*

The Los Positas Literary Anthology: *Evermore and Goodbye Again*

Minerva Rising: *Entering the Space*

Uncertain Promise Anthology: *Our Ventana* (2nd place winner)

Contents

Gratitudes

Collecting these essays, written over the span of fourteen years, brings back moments with people who fledged this book into life. With gratitude I thank John Parsley, for publishing Honeymoons (he gave me wings); Jon Varese and Sofie Kleppner my diehard readers through many early drafts. The Goddard inspirations: Michael Klein, Elena Georgiou and Beatrix Gates. Jeffrey Levine for polishing my poetics and Kristina Marie Darling for being the intrepid KMD. Lise Goett for running me through poetic marathons and challenging the fine points of my prose. The incisive and thoughtful Geoffrey Gatza.

I am forever grateful.

To the generations before ours,
and those that follow.
And to this day; Kai, Julia, Ashley, Nima,
Michael,
and Doug forever.

UNDERSTANDING MOONSEED
ESSAYS OF LIFE

Sixteen Chakras

I was a wreck, couldn't get my head to my left shoulder. I had a massage that reached bits.

1.

There was a window above the bathroom sink. It opened pantry-style, a deep shelf pushing out to freezing Chicago winters. My mother stored our dairy products on the shelf, opening the window's door to food stored on a two-foot ledge before the screen in place to keep out summertime mosquitos. Most often the dairy products were ice. I remember that the tiny refrigerator in the kitchen worked, and wonder. Was madness at play in this placement of food or is it better explained by saying that my mother let me experience what she grew up with: an "icebox?"

2.

For some reason, I was born a Democrat. Odd from a solidly Republican set of parents. They fought, except in politics where they agreed in different cities, voting for different local candidates. I managed to disagree in either city. So at seven, I stood at the corner of Cedar and State Street, handing out JFK bumper stickers with my whole heart in the act. Sometime later in the campaign, I slithered between shiny shoes and heavy coats lining a velvet rope between brass stands at the Conrad Hilton to shake the hand of JFK, his big digits stretching over my hand quickly before reaching out to others.

3.

MaryAnne MacFarlane was the assistant to the headmaster, an astute Irish lesbian who took a liking to me even though I dropped her typing class in high school after deciding that good typing qualified a girl for a lesser job. It was a big decision. Somehow she stuck around in the wings of my rocky, high-school experience, swooping in after my best show of drama with a message. "You're not fooling anyone but yourself."

4.

   I love music. There was the kind produced by my tiny hands that started piano at five and continued until liberated by a friend who drove us to football games in the suburbs in her father's convertible with diplomatic plates. The music of others tore into my heart, filling me, setting off hopes, questions, conviction. But my lessons raged on until the day a sour teacher assigned me the very piece I had played in my audition for him. I loved the piece and the reprieve, didn't have to practice. He knew what he was doing and fired me.

5.

   My father lived in New York, and I did not. My mother declared a seven-year war in which I did not see him, even for tiny visits. Her ceasefire when I was sixteen was more of a total capitulation, "I'm sending her to you"—"to fix," her unspoken message. I met a stepmother, a half sister, and a half brother. More family than I'd ever had, and they had families. These were the people inside the windows I looked through at Christmas. My father had suffered more heart attacks than one could count; he lived, grumpy from meds, fierce in conviction that his reincarnation was imminent. I fantasized that we made the fruitcake aging in the cupboard, together, father and daughter. He told me, "Cut out the bullshit" and bragged about having big balls.

6.

   The icebox-bathroom had a cupboard high above the toilet. (This was an odd place, don't you think?) I climbed on the toilet, reaching into the cupboard to get to the letters kept in boxes. Late at night, I'd find my mother working through those letters, reading, the boxes in her lap. I was a shadow, spying and fading, learning my own story in darkness. I climbed up and took down the boxes when she was away. Saul Nack. Child support. Missed payments. Failure. Custody. I looked up the words, and then went on a search. How does one get to be a parent? I found the word: "sperm."

7.

  The Democrats lived large and powerful in Chicago under Mayor Richard J. Daley, a name that must be said in its entirety. Mayor Richard J. Daley and I had the same dentist, and I saw him rather often in my high school years in the elevator to the office of Dr. Phillips. We'd smile at each other and chat. He knew I was a Dem, and I thought he'd make one of the best Santas I'd ever seen and perhaps a really good dad. Dr. Phillips was another story, having worked with Albert Schweitzer and devised clever ideas like using drill bits to fill root canals before the high-tech age of cat gut. I've had some drill bits in my root canals from my early days of chewing too much Juicy Fruit and drinking Coke. It's thrilling to be in a chair now when a dentist says in awe, "Oh my, tell me about what I'm seeing." I'm connected to history.

8.

  I love the name Paddy Whannel and enjoyed his college film classes. Those were the coming-to-terms years. I also had a professor named Alan Artner who assigned readings in John Abbott McNeill Ruskin's *The Gentle Art of Making Enemies.* Alan and I dated. He wanted to sleep with me in the worst way. He had really bad teeth. Paddy Whannel handed back a paper that said, "You've got more to give than this." I got the message. Although I had taken up acting under the tutelage of Leigh Roloff and Lila Heston, acting terrified me. For all that I feared, I imagined a saw carving a circle in the floor around my feet. The circle complete, I would drop through, out of the sight, safe.

10.

  Here's how I joined the NAACP. It was sixth grade, in an exclusive private school in a converted mansion with a regal entry staircase—and the usual, nasty back one for the servants. The school's students used both. The servant staircase was a meeting ground for kisses, lingering chats, hoping for kisses, and dashes hoping never to confront the conversation. I stopped one day, meeting the dark eyes of Stephen Wade. He insisted on having his name spoken in its entirety and spelled out the "ph" when introducing himself. His brother was an over-achiever at the University of Chicago. One Monday morning he announced, "My brother joined the NAACP, and I did, too." He boasted a very appealing metal button on the lapel of his uniform jacket. I desperately, all of a sudden, wanted to make sure that every human had opportunity, perhaps including me, though I didn't think of that at the time. My heart went out to every Black person, every civil rights march that I had already attended, and for the lips of Stephen Wade, who has since made a name as a banjo player.

11.

　　Just before I started high school, I decided my mother and I needed to move. I toured apartments in our neighborhood and found one in a six-plex once occupied by Hemingway. My mother signed the lease with no comment. The apartment's hardwood floors were a little warped in places but three bedrooms made it seem normal in every respect except that my mother slept under the dining room table. I was otherwise quite proud of the dining room. It was a good place, though we never once ate there. When my friends stopped by, still hallucinating from a bad trip, my mother served strawberries and tea in the living room. On two occasions, my house was the last stop before they were taken away for treatment of persistent flashbacks.

14.

　　I was always the youngest in the class. It wasn't until many years later that I realized I simply did not get what went on all around me in high school. One friend, sexually abused by her brother and a cousin, battled a mother in denial by stealing her tranquilizers. Another couldn't shake flashbacks, and I was dispatched with a kitten to lure her into the car that would take her to the hospital. The local pharmacy assistant, my boyfriend, was a drug dealer who claimed his dad had invented the drinking straw. He died in a car accident some years later in the grip of whatever drug. Our local brand- name heiress took off on a cross-country junket–a well-funded, druggy boondoggle with a boyfriend who needed a cause. Many years later I found the report from a shrink who evaluated me. He wrote, "I would caution anyone who takes this girl as a patient: look beyond her sophisticated presentation. She came into my office, smoking using a cigarette holder. At the end of our session, she asked if I could lend her money for cigarettes."

15.

　　In college, the study of acting was useful in many ways, one being that it taught me how to breathe. Acting class started with lying on the floor, palms on our diaphragms feeling our breath. Shoulders still, chest still, the lower ribs opened as the diaphragm worked, pulling oxygen into the lowest recesses of the lungs. It was calming, centering. In my days of anxiety attacks and the nights when they became insomnia, I'd feel my stomach tight and hard, my chest heaving in hyperventilation. The floor became my remedy, the cloud that lifted me, palm on diaphragm, carrying me through space and time to sanity, sleep, peace.

16.

I still forget the thing that works better than holding every little thing inside, the worries, sadness and fears. My massage therapist calls me rebar, and unbends the tightness. My therapist embraces a tangled bundle, and sets strands of me straight. I'm learning to let go, inhale deep in the recesses of stomach and soul. I'm learning that seeking is not finding, but exhaling just might be.

JFK and Me

I must have taken people by surprise, a seven-year-old standing alone on the corner of Cedar and State Street, passing out bumper stickers and campaign buttons for JFK. It was an act of irony and early independence as I was born into a solidly Republican family, their tradition marred only by the fact that my mother once voted for FDR—and now me. "Passing out" understates my zeal; I was determined to get a button on every lapel in motion, to undermine the integrity of gleaming chrome with that red, white, and blue strip featuring the name Kennedy and his irresistible smiling face.

I look back on his campaign slogan, *Leadership for the '60s,* with today's hindsight on all that I did not know about him then, I don't think I would change my seven-year-old stance. At the time, I was so much a fan (was it really my first crush on an older man?), that when he came to the Conrad Hilton as president in March of 1963, I managed to slither my ten-year-old frame between the camel hairs and lesser winter coats right up to the rope aisle and stanchions to shake his hand. The occasion that day was a civic luncheon where he identified unemployment as a national economic concern specifically related to youth workers, agriculture, and automation. Eight short months later, he would be dead.

My mother, a puritanical persona who artfully concealed the parts of her that were not prudish, hinted to me in age-appropriate innuendos that Kennedy was not a saint. Even then I knew what that meant. She went on to say that he could never be effective without Bobby and crowned her indictment, saying that he was in cahoots with the Mafia. She did, however, shed tears when little premature Patrick died and complimented Mrs. Kennedy on being "such a lady" before launching into a hissed vilification of a rich socialite from money marrying money. When Bobby went after organized crime and, as historical record shows, redirected the president from his bromance with Frank Sinatra, I took a victory lap in loud and vigorous debate with my mother. Somehow, Marilyn Monroe singing "Happy Birthday Mr. President" just didn't spark my interest.

My private school in a converted mansion at the edge of Lincoln Park required my mother to drive me from our Gold Coast apartment on her way to the north- side high school where she taught English literature. Car time was say-what's-on-your-mind-time (a strategy I would like to think I later employed with better results with my own daughters). Driving through April's showers in 1961, I heard a lot about the Bay of Pigs from my mother because it turns out that one thing worse than being a Democrat was being a Communist, and Castro definitely was a Communist (of course completely a puppet of Khrushchev), which meant that the CIA most definitely *should* have prevailed, and it was *just terrible, just awful,* that this attempt at setting the world order right had failed. And now the Communists knew about our plot against them and that would endanger the Cold War world order even further, so it was a good thing that we have air-raid shelters. In case something awful happened.

I was developing anxiety and also getting a hint of how fact and fear can coexist on a collision course.

It's not surprising that my mother told me point-blank that we were getting into another world war a year and a half later when the story broke that the Soviets had shipped nuclear missiles to Cuba that were capable of attacking US cities. History offers a better set of facts than my very nervous mother who scared the shit out of me every morning in the car. Turns out that through a Russian spy masquerading as a clown performing for children in the Kennedy compound, Bobby established a back-channel to craft a secret deal with the Russian ambassador whereby America would pull out of Turkey and Soviet weapons would be withdrawn from Cuba. My mother and I were not the only ones who were greatly relieved.

Today especially, I want to vote for a president who comes from principles of service to the people and the nation. Subsequent generations have shown the Kennedys to have plenty of that, along with the tragedy and human failings that have kept us all riveted for almost seventy years.

There was no PA system in my mansion-school. The news of JFK's assassination travelled floor to floor and classroom to classroom, carried by breathless students that November 22nd. Like so many, I was riveted to the black-and-white broadcast of the motorcade, the salute, the veil over Jackie's face. The hours after the assassination replayed Johnson's swearing in next to Jackie's blood-stained suit, and history has since exposed all the ways that JFK was not a saint. But JFK had our backs.

Life In Architecture

I was born in the city of Bauhaus black buildings, Mies Van Der Rohe skyscrapers along a lake that sometimes shimmered with metallic elway corpses washing ashore—a city famous for the wedding cake Robie brick house and the horizontal lines of Frank Lloyd Wright.

Within a world of tall limestone, I lived in an apartment half in the ground, walked broken sidewalks to a stone church, then to a mansion-school with a circular staircase to bedrooms-turned-classrooms, and then to a brick high school with an asphalt yard and cinder-block, converted coach house.

Next, I matriculated to a frozen lakefront campus, where salt and snow again whitened months of the year until spring greened stone structures with ivy. There in a brick four-plex on Reba Street I found love with my boy/man, his Jesus curls, beard and mustache. His facial hair went, he stayed.

He drove his Fiat to California. We moved to our stucco apartment on Wildwood, then our stucco house on Mauricia and last our boxcar house on Highland.

We rebuilt Highland with columns and recessed lighting on bright art—threw parties in primary colors for people in lipsticked smiles and handshakes built of four hands. We bore two daughters, and our exuberant girls greeted everyone with hugs and sloppy kisses. We ran businesses showcased in pages of advertising and pastel circuit plots showing components that would be miniaturized into a microchip to be manufactured by people made indistinct in white suits and masks.

Fluffy blonde curls and scarecrow-white strands distinguished the two girls in the family that rested in a lakefront redwood cabin, rode up snowy slopes and schussed down, hiked dusty trails with dogs dashing between boulders and humans, rocked in a lakeside hammock breathing the smell of burning logs, as snow melted by the fire inside avalanched from the roof to the ground.

And then a moment in a jumbled office filled with paper—files about people— and new words about them, about him. Words with a hollow, haunting sound of diagnosis. I was there, he was. In these white walls.

New yellow limestone. Hardwood and flagstone, skylights and harp music as if a dream. Up stone stairs, wide, white doors, rounded chairs, sterile surround. A steady beep as drugs were infused into his veins, our foundation newly built of hope and hopelessness, and the two of us together.

With solid certainty, death lurked at life's flimsy frame. The structure we thought sound was neither limestone, granite, wood, stucco, or even a sturdy tent. Love was the wind in daylight, barely touching our skin as we passed under a brilliant sun.

Flight To The Future

On February 15, 1975, I checked a couple of suitcases at Chicago's O'Hare Airport and boarded the United 727 that would take me to a new life with Doug who had driven out weeks earlier and found our new home in a town quaintly named Sunnyvale. Because one traveled, in those days, in dressy attire, I flew in a double-breasted linen suit, seated next to a dark-haired guy in a silk-blend suit. The words "Silicon Valley" had no meaning for me.

The move west at age twenty-two challenged my growing-up assumption that I would live in New York. Yet I was in love, and Doug had gone some weeks earlier to get established.

There was a sense of destiny about this move to California. The summer before, I had graduated from college. Doug had quit his job as a junior engineer in a Chicago-based instrumentation company. It was a hard-won position he obtained a year earlier —in spite of his degree in film production—by displaying circuit boards of his own design from his latest synthesizer, the fifth he had designed and built. Although the presence of a keyboard gave the look of a familiar instrument, the functionality of knobs, colorful patch cords and faders made it look very complicated. Synthesizers could bend, hiss and resonate rumbles that were entirely unlike the sound of striking a piano key.

After quitting his job, Doug had taken some weeks off to enter a contest co-sponsored by *Electronic Design* magazine with a company called InterDesign. The contest challenge: to make custom connections on the final layer of a microchip that would complete the layers below, demonstrating a simplified approach to designing an integrated circuit. Doug entered the contest with a voltage-controlled oscillator design that could reduce the size of yet another of his synthesizers. His sights set on the hundred chips he would be awarded if he won, he submitted his entry, and we took off on a cross-country junket that began in New York and wended down the east coast.

In a call to his parents from Atlanta, I heard him say, "Who? Who's that? OK, what's his phone number?"

He cradled the phone against his shoulder as he dialed the next call. "I'm returning a call from ..."

His brown eyes widened behind slightly tinted lenses of wire-rimmed aviator glasses.

"Yes, I am Doug Curtis. Yes? Really? When? Well, I'm traveling right now, and I won't be back for a week or so. I could…."

I listened, enjoying the crisp air conditioning against my skin, no longer sticky in the smothering humidity outside. Doug said a final, "Ok," and "I'll call you then," and returned the receiver to the payphone's hook.

"I won. I get my VCO chips!"

"Fantastic." I loved how happy he was, yet a little part of me held back with some strong sense that this would change our lives.

"They're giving me an HP scientific calculator, and they want me to come to California."

"When are you going to do that?" I had visions of hightailing it back to the Midwest so he could go right away.

"I told them I'd call when I was done traveling."

We continued our trip for ten more days, driving north into Canada to visit friends before returning home. Doug flew to California and returned with his chips, his new calculator, and a photo of him holding his circuit diagram.

"They offered me a job."

Anxiety took hold of me. Move to California? "What did you say?"

"I told them I wanted to build my new synthesizer."

Months later, the synthesizer built, a recession had set in.

"They keep calling me to come work for them." A few days later I heard the words I had been expecting, "I said yes. I'll drive out at the end of the month."

That was January.

Just as Doug had "won" his first career position, destiny seemed to help me find a job as a writer/producer in a film production company. A year later I moved to a copy/contact position in a San Francisco-based technology-advertising agency. Our clients were minicomputer and chip companies—and terminal manufacturers. Those were the days when the "terminal" was a distant appendage to the mainframe or emerging mini-computer that centralized all intelligence.

At the ripe old age of twenty-four—just two years and two jobs after moving to California—I started my own "company" with an art director in an office that we shared.

For a time we were independent entities—Mary A. Pacifico, Writer and Keoki Williams Design. Then we were Delicious Advertising using Keoki's signature pineapple logo. A couple years into our fledgling business, I decided to make a run for the "big-time," which meant becoming a full-service agency with consistent clients, not just projects. It took some courage to put my name on the door, but it was the perfect West coast name: Pacifico.

In Silicon Valley, young people started companies, unlike New York where I had expected to become an entrepreneur when older and with credible grey hair.

Although I started Pacifico, Inc. with consumer clients–performing arts, car dealerships, a shopping center, banks, restaurants—I was surrounded by technology, had some experience with it, and I lived with the perfect technology coach. I hired a few employees and sought out Silicon Valley companies, taking on a semiconductor foundry, and clients that made test devices, capital equipment focused on the semiconductor market, enterprise software and military electronics. As Silicon Valley grew, Pacifico grew its client and revenue base.

Doug was my biggest supporter. "You have nothing to lose. You can always get a real job."

He repeated this with a funny grin. Both of us knew I most certainly could not work any harder for another employer than I already did for my own clients.

I, in turn, thought it was easy stuff—hard work, but I was suited to running my own company. "Everyone should start their own business."

Some friends took my advice only to return to jobs in other companies. Two years after I started Pacifico, Doug fulfilled what I always knew he would do, founding Curtis Electromusic Specialties. He designed signal processing chips for almost all the major synthesizer brands in the world, producing an "analog sound" that was sought by rock 'n' roll musicians. With his chip technology packed onto circuit boards, synthesizers became sleeker, looking more like keyboards with lights and knobs. Side by side, we entered the Silicon Valley lifestyle, working our separate long hours in a valley of long hours and game-changing innovation.

I found that for every Gordon Moore and Andy Grove of Intel fame, there were hundreds of talented and very detail-oriented engineers and physicists, albeit uncelebrated, who created a new world on the largest scale by focusing their efforts on the smallest scale. Silicon wafers, the real estate on which chips were manufactured, got larger and larger, creating demand for manufacturing systems that could handle these bigger silicon slices. The components etched onto the wafers became smaller with more minute geometries, the densely packed equivalent of shrinking the room-sized computer of my high-school career onto a single circuit board and eventually onto a pencil eraser-sized chip.

My clients were founders, innovators, fast trackers, detail geeks, venture capitalists and inventors who sometimes thought their technical prowess qualified them to do anything—including what I did. I sometimes quipped to Doug, "Just let me know if you'd like my help on your next IC."

He'd answer with that crooked grin and tell me he'd like some help now. That settled, we'd do whatever we were doing next.

Apple was a fledgling company at the time Pacifico got its start. Software as a tool got pushed from enterprise-only to the small business to the individual. Renegade companies like Atari and Pizza Time Theater moved games from the traditional coffee table board to the restaurant and then the device.

Still fresh is the moment some years later when a colleague said to me, "Our old test-equipment client is migrating to an internet company." At the time, the Internet was the communication vehicle for research types. He went on to say, "They're going to use the internet for commerce."

"This could be huge—if it works," I thought to myself. We quickly reset their corporate identity focus from printed letterhead to the computer screen, and produced a suite of branding materials. The changes wrought by the internet escalated from internal communication to ecommerce, email for all, online retailing, and eventually, social media.

Change converged from every corner of my world in the form of new business models based on networked enterprises and wireless connectivity that rippled into specific applications and problems that needed new solutions—like security. I embraced it all, honchoing every new opportunity for my organization, which grew to one of the largest independent integrated-marketing communication firms in Silicon Valley. We took on global tech clients: the world's largest wafer foundry, three global semiconductor capital equipment suppliers, leaders in internet security, the company that pioneered standards for motion-picture theaters and later home entertainment; and then, a succession of internet-based businesses focused on home purchases and loans, engineering components, a commercial building portal, online purchasing, and collaboration.

Pacifico had to hold the doors shut, and I felt like an air traffic controller graphing out our workload to make sure I didn't stress our increasingly youthful staff. I hired in ways I never had, the motto being "redundancy." Headhunters called endlessly, pitching stock options to the young ones who could fog a mirror, but had no experience. They jumped to the next opportunity, the stock options, like lemmings. It moved at a dizzying pace.

I was sustained by a new kind of client call. "I have two million dollars to create this brand. Do you have bandwidth?"

Just a few years earlier I had lamented to Doug, "You have leverage that an agency doesn't. You can shut down a manufacturing line, if they don't get your chips."

He didn't miss the chance to point out now, "This a new time for the ad/pr biz." He was right. For a brief and fleeting moment, I had the leverage to say yes or no to the client. Hiring was another story; the business had to compete for its people.

Convened for an activity called SPAM—something personal about me—the newbies in the company joined with the oldtimers to exchange stories about themselves. We got to know each other, started liking our differences, started feeling like a team and then the famous bubble burst. Slashed budgets and corporate uncertainty became the new way of life. The robust advertising and public relations agency that I had built spiraled downward.

Gone were the days of multi-million dollar print, radio and television campaigns, calling journalists to pitch a story; man-on-the-street market research, and afternoons on the golf course with prospective or current clients.

Those days went the way of the Mergenthaler typesetting machine, photostats, rubylith, art boards, bluelines, color separations, conference reports, calls to action, production artists, airbrushed photos, mag tape, answer prints, cut-and-splice editing shops and distributing materials for publication or broadcast by shipping them to radio/TV stations or publications around the country. All of these things became extinct, obviated into the ether. Photoshop became both a noun and a verb, taking its place in the hall of fame of reusable parts of speech along with Hoover, ketchup,

FedEx, and Xerox. We Photoshopped any image to make wholesale changes to landscapes, backgrounds, facial expressions, and more minor details.

With email we could cc and bcc as many people as many times a day as we could stomach. To send materials, we emailed a wav file for broadcast, a pdf or jpeg file unless the pubs wanted tiff or eps format. The media receiving our stuff were increasingly online anyway, and what we sent got compressed to a banner that winked onscreen. No business was real without a dynamic Web presence.

I lived in the capital of change, Silicon Valley, and experienced firsthand some of the most dramatic change in the history of my own industry.

9/11 hit like a punch to an already depressed economy that reeled from the lesson of funding half-baked wunderkind product ideas that were not worthy of being called companies. In the empty skies that followed 9/11, a terrorist took hold as the game changer and a silence took over for a time. Then, cautious marketers with budgets in tight fists turned to closed-loop marketing with its immediate lead generation benefits. A sales force could take over without the traditional human interaction that once warmed up the sale. If the online prospect took one single action, clicking on a specific topic or link on a banner, webinar or web page, that action was recorded, sent to a database. Follow-up email relevant to the action would be sent without human intervention to the action-taker or the person who needs to follow up. It's fast, cheap and virtual.

Our clients newly counted on us to make their products viral, a term that had meaning beyond the notion of contagion. Viral was code for free.

Just about the only thing that didn't change was that advertising and public relations are about people and money, because only people form perceptions and only people can spend the money on products and services. People write the stories about these products and services, whether they're posted to a blog or jotted on your grandmother's tired, old fish wrap. People contribute to reputation by talking to one another, carrying on great oral traditions just as Native Americans passed on their wisdom about the animals, the stars and the Way. We tell each other about the deal, the sale, the manufacturing defect, what the latest thing is and who just got it. That's not a perception. It's the reality of our biz: eventually people have to meet, look each other in the eye, talk, agree or disagree, and take action.

Only much later did I realize how true it is that some things just don't change— including some sticky memories.

Once when we talked about the future, Doug said cancer would get him, and I replied that heart would get me. We couldn't know, but it was almost as if we did in those early years. We would forget that conversation until a new future appeared: a pain, a moment, a mass, a careening detour from all that we had created and looked forward to together. Suddenly in a disease-defined time capsule, finite in measure we did not know, a story of love would become one of loss, transformation and survival.

On that flight on the 15th of February in 1975, a young woman with long, auburn hair and almond-shaped, green eyes sat next to a dark-eyed stranger in a silk-blend suit. The plane bounced and rattled through clear skies over the Rockies, more turbulence than that young woman had experienced ever in her years of flying. She turned to the stranger, wildly anxious, and he said, "It will help you to place your hand over mine, but don't grab. Simply let your hand rest flat on mine."

She looked into his eyes, wondered about what was ahead and laid her hand palm-down over the top of the hand he spread on the plastic armrest between them. Sunlight shone through the plane's oblong windows.

Honeymoons

A wedding took place in our Los Gatos home on January 2, 1982, a day when heavy rain washed out creeks, killed twenty-nine people and caused hillsides and houses to slip onto major roads. Oblivious to the destruction, we admired the roiling clouds over our deck. Doug's mother, two years into brain cancer, sat front row center, next to my mother whose hair was the auburn of Ronald Reagan's. The best man, newly a father, stood proud next to Doug; his wife and newborn son resting in a guest bedroom. It was a day following ten years of living together thinking that we were too young or too busy to marry—ten years graduating from college, moving across country, buying houses, starting businesses, making new friends and traveling as lovers and best friends. It was a day, ten years into our life together, that marked the beginning of our twenty-five year search for the perfect honeymoon.

After the wedding, during our short honeymoon in Carmel, a storm blew smoke back through the fireplace chimney into our seaside room. The couple next door seemed alternately horrified and thrilled.

"Oh, help, help!" He was well over six feet tall, dark, with steel-blue eyes, running through a hallway that constrained him to a few steps before turning back and turning again. A scarf around his head tied into a bow on top would have completed the gait. His booming voice seemed to keep him in motion.

Stopped in our path, his slight, blonde partner panicked. "Do you think the smoke could kill us?"

Doug smiled. "Open your window just a little to let the smoke out of your room. Don't open it all the way."

We returned to our room, and I slid out of my satin nightgown. Smoke, wind, and rain slapping our windows, nighttime and the sweet touch of my husband made our honeymoon. We both agreed that we would continue to search for the perfect honeymoon: one of leisurely weeks, days filled with nature, and celebration of newness before us.

Over the years we traveled to Hawaii, each time saying we were previewing honeymoon locations. Doug made travel arrangements.

"We'll have a balcony overlooking the ocean, and I made sure the bedroom is on the water so we can listen to the waves." He had specific requirements and assured them with sparking, brown eyes.

"Sweetheart, come see. I made this sunset for you." His baritone voice called me, taking credit for crimson swatches against pink and orange. When I reached his side he glowed. "What do you think?"

"This one may be the best yet."

It was our game, our promise to keep looking. On our Cayman Island dive trip I was mildly seasick much of the time. Dolphins leapt on each side of our bow for miles as we crossed from island to island. Landside, magenta flame trees offered fleeting shade as we puttered on mopeds.

This was the trip where Doug's dive buddy stood on fish parts cut to attract the three eight-foot nurse sharks that now circled the divers below the boat. I heard the story when they came up and later saw the episode on videotape, a story that fed my fear of scuba diving.

"Give it a try." As Doug urged me on, I looked at Stuart, our dive master, who reviewed basic dive tables with me and then promised, as my buddy, to keep me on a measured descent and ascent. Doug beat us off the side of the boat.

My legs floated out, tossing me into a lounge position, my feet parallel to my ears. That was the funniest thing. "Oh no," in my brain, I giggled. "Nitrogen narcosis at twenty-five feet."

I adjusted to the oxygen tank pulling me backward and looked through sunlit water at mute coral reefs and a scattering of fish in ruby, cobalt, golden and charcoal. It was the world I expected to see rendered strange by sun beaming through water, shafts of light electrifying every particle before me, then shifting, a soft mosaic as the surface tide whispered toward the shore. Darting, hungry fish glimmered into this mosaic, stopping to pull at the coral, then chewed with painted, tropical lips in a sound I heard ever so faintly like distant potato chips, a crunch just beyond reach, but real. I heard a world I had never imagined.

Doug fluttered eel-like to peek under coral and between rocks. Stuart led, but Doug narrated, beckoning me on to see a shy octopus, slimy sea cucumbers, starfish, and morays hidden, awake for a strike.

"That was easy—and beautiful!" Back on deck I felt accomplished.

"You did fine. But there's so much more to see when you're in deeper water in the open ocean. There are many more little creatures and fish that don't come this close to shore." The words spilled out of him.

Doug designed microchips that created and shaped the sounds produced by electronic music synthesizers that became a major part of the rock 'n' roll of the late seventies to early nineties. Doug's chips had started to play a major role in most synthesizer brands. Music industry meetings dominated his Tokyo agenda. Taking the Shinkansen Express to Hamamatsu, we bulleted through misty countryside. glimpsing blue-tiled, upward-turning roofs that distinguished ordinary stucco houses. We arrived for more meetings, soon to reboard the train to Kyoto, then a taxi to our ryokan. Cross-legged on cushions over tatami mats, we sat in low light with a high sense of discovery, eating kaiseki of pickled vegetables, sashimi, and tempura.

"When in Japan…." Doug directed his answer to me rather than the smiling, bowing older man who arrived at our doorway. The old man set down a basket of soaps and towels and turned on steaming hot water. We knew one didn't soap in the tiny square tub, so we took turns soaping, rinsing, and then soaking. Deep heat penetrated our flesh and being, sleep overtook us, and we woke to sunlight warming us in a simple, beautiful place.

"I love this, but it's not quite a honeymoon," we said to one another.

On our many trips to Europe, most places disqualified themselves for a honeymoon. There was so much to do and see, but London didn't have sunsets or the sweeping vistas. Holland and Germany were all business—trade shows, meetings with music-industry customers and partners, all under dark skies. The forest where I ran was sparse with stringy trees. Business continued in Italy until we broke for vacation in Rome, Florence and Venice, just cities. Doug had a bad experience many years earlier, and he shied away from France, but our trip there with our girls one year was a nod to the business of educating our children.

There were honeymoon moments in Europe: a flat with plump, stuffed furniture overlooking the Thames, our first stop on our first trip to Europe together some years before we married. I fell asleep after a cup of tea, to awaken pink with contentment in his arms until the jolt.

"Sweetheart, we can't sleep in the middle of the day. We have to be in this time zone."

In Cinque Terra, we hiked the mountain path that linked five little towns; lingered at beaches sprinkled with bikinis, nudes, and multilingual chatter; and wandered each little town narrating local history to one another. By night we scrutinized food displays and menus before choosing a restaurant for dinner.

I'm not sure Doug claimed any of the sunsets to be of his making. Though history and hiking were rich in many places, but none announced itself as our honeymoon spot.

One year, arm in arm in a pristine German train, I remember looking up at Doug, studying his sleepy profile, He thought his nose was big; I thought it was strong. His upper lip arched farther from the center than usual, calling attention to his thin mouth. His jawline angled from chin to ear. Savoring every detail including an ear lobe with a tiny cleft, I inserted myself into his sleep. "I love traveling together."

He awoke momentarily to kiss me and closed his eyes. Airplanes and trains always put him to sleep.

Europe was just too busy for our honeymoon. We both agreed on that.

On a catamaran trip in the Bahamas, I was newly pregnant and didn't scuba. Doug brought me orange juice and toast, took turns diving with friends, and then snorkeling with me. We free dove under rays with ten-foot wingspans, glimpsing their almost human faces. Doug stayed close, as barracudas lurked in a semicircle just below the water's surface.

"Sweetheart, it's not you they like. It's your jewelry."

At night, we admired his sunsets and each other.

"Let's start our children swimming early, so they can scuba dive when they're teenagers. I can't wait to show them what many people never see, all the creatures in their natural habitat."

Our first child fulfilled a dream that for a time seemed impossible until, in an instant as sudden as all those when there was no life within me, I was pregnant. Soon that word meant nausea and hunger in equal measures and then, just as the nausea subsided, I felt tiny butterfly wings against my stomach growing stronger and stronger, the gentle beating of wings in flight, cells building upon cells to create our child.

But first, I took on the appearance of a woman with a basketball carelessly concealed under specially designed clothes, and all, including me would pronounce, "It's a boy." The butterfly basketball got so large that round parts of it suddenly protruded like oversized boils moving from side to side as if my stomach was taking itself for a walk. The life inside me ran out of room exactly one week ahead of schedule.

By the first light one day, I couldn't sleep. Writhing from one position to another, I was awake from a pressing pain in my back. He-who-never-wore-a-watch asked for a watch and said, "It seems to be coming every three minutes."

Timing the pain had not occurred to me, but now calling the doctor did. An on-call doc returned our message. "You can go to the hospital, if you like. They'll look at you and probably send you home. You're a first timer. You don't know."

I thought to myself, "This doctor doesn't know me—"

Backing out our long driveway, Doug first hit the bushes on one side and a car on the other side, then settled down for the short drive to the hospital. Check-in, transfer to a room, a quick examination and then came the verdict. "We're keeping you. You're in labor."

When the nurse wheeled in a machine that graphed my contractions, Doug took his position monitoring the tracing and warning me when the next one was close. We breathed together.

"This woman cannot push out a baby of this size." A new verdict after hours of pushing and signs of fetal distress. I was quickly wheeled into the operating room where a team numbed me, prepped me for a C-section, placed Doug beside me, and began tugging at me as if pulling the meat out of a tight sausage casing. Someone dropped the curtain before my face, revealing a little Buddha, damp and confused, squinting in the light. Soon we held our first child, our ten-pound baby girl, our Ashley.

Together we learned of another kind of love affair, the one as parents with our child, a love that transformed us in ways that seemed obvious, but could not be foretold. Only Doug—a man who rarely held babies—only this tender man could soothe Ashley's colic in a way of his own invention, carrying her face down, straddle-legged on his arm like a giant football, red-faced and loud for the short time until his gentle rocking put her to sleep. Only I seemed to have an endless list of nicknames and songs for her new expressions and sounds. The Ashley song: "A-S-H-L-E-Y. Ashley that's me." She responded with big, china-blue eyes, a serious gaze, "Sure, Mom. I'll learn my name. I'll learn how to spell at six weeks." Soon she started wrestling with the giant bears lining her crib, and I was pregnant again. And then, just as suddenly, there was blood and no heartbeat where there had been one. I miscarried before Christmas. More tiny clothes and toys appeared for Ashley as Santa added a new house to his route—ours. I read that nature took the ones who were not forming properly—what was meant to be. Ashley bounced, scooted around pulling pots and pans out of the cupboard, said her first word, "hot." We hung on her every movement, parents utterly in love.

Two weeks after New Year's Eve in 1991, I was again pregnant—fearful, thankfully sick and hungry and full of the hope only known to those vessels that gain their meaning and fulfillment by carrying a life. Soon enough I felt the butterflies start gently within, but then a different sensation: tiny fingertips probing, pushing lightly in places within me, exploring the world from within.

I got the basketball look soon enough again, and though all said, "It's a boy," I knew only two things. This was a very different personality, and it was a girl.

The three of us traveled to Hawaii for a gardenia-scented, ocean-rhythm rest before the final trimester. Returning home, I lay down for a nap and two-year-old Ashley tossed herself alongside me, pitching her arm over my belly where a pronounced kick from within landed itself against my belly and into Ashley's harsh arm.

On the appointed day, I had my car washed and drove myself to the hospital with Doug in the passenger seat, Ashley firmly buckled into her toddler seat, braced for the scheduled C-section. An hour later, an eight-and-a-half-pound redheaded girl with perfect lips and wide, cobalt eyes lay across my chest, gazing at me with the wisdom of the womb as if to say, "So this is the other side."

We had our Julia. Our family complete, we added her to our eternal love affair.

Our girls hiked at our mountain cabin and camped on trips in our new minivan. One year we drove to Death Valley on a route that took us to tufa towers, ghostly monuments of Mono Lake. The girls darted between the misshapen spires before climbing into the van to be entertained by choruses from a six-pack of Disney tapes.

We spent an afternoon at altitude 8,375 feet, in the abandoned town of Bodie. Peering into saloon windows, an upstairs bedroom, a dusty church, we saw the desperation of flight from a town overrun with thieves. Two-and-a-half-year-old Julia sputtered stories of her own making about "the bad boys from Bodie."

Closing in on our destination, occasional Joshua trees against rocky hillsides lured us; craggy hints, darkening colors drew us closer to Death Valley's varied beauty.

We reached the only point on Earth that stretches from 282 feet below sea level to over 11,000 high, where stone formations in golden, turquoise and fuschia are named Artists Pallette, white salt flats shimmer in sunlight at Zabriskie Point; white persists in shadowed, lumpy formations on the Devil's Golf Course. Sidewinder tracks marred windswept dunes; roadrunners screeched and jerked across our paths. We hiked in 108-degree sunlit canyons, Julia seated comfortably in the pack on my back.

We felt a reverence for this place, knowing nothing of its native Panamint Shoshone; their gatherings to dance, play games, and hear storytellers pass on the history of the world, animals and People. We knew none of that nor of the "red-rock face paint" their ancestors used in their ceremonies, colors from their land. Did the spirits of this land sit with us here?

Leaning back after a camp dinner, filled with well-being under stars crowding across the sky, I said to Doug, "We work so hard for our lifestyle, but look where we come for contentment."

Sitting together on Death Valley's immense floor, we surveyed crowded pinpoints that threatened to spill out of a brimming sky, knowing that fledgling stars waited to appear exactly where the spilt ones started. We breathed deeply together as we had between contractions, this time watching our little girls sleep, here in a sandy desert, outside our tent simply sitting, together. "It's kind of a family honeymoon," he said.

Ashley and Julia grew; theater, soccer, basketball, volleyball and water polo pulled Doug and me in different directions, sometimes to different cities and parts of the country. Doug added rugged, ten-day hikes with our nephews in scenic places I would have loved minus the rigor of their vertical climb: the Grand Tetons, the Olympic Mountains, the Milford Trail and Machu Picchu. A younger nephew took charge of scheduling these trips, always it seemed, at times when our family had layered sets of plans and activities with me left to manage. Never consulted in advance, I wallowed in resentment and complained angrily. It all rolled off Doug. "In one ear, out the other," his mother once said of him. He came home from each trip tired, happy to see us, stepping easily into the pace of our life.

In later years he added in heli-skiing trips to Kicking Horse and Snowbird, biking/camping in Moab, and rondonee skiing on any backcountry slope with snow. He lived his passion for nature; it made him healthy, vibrant, the man I loved more deeply than ever. I felt a dawning happiness that he packed his life, feeding his passion the way devoutly religious people absorb scripture.

We traveled as a family to Zion, Bryce and the Grand Canyon, Telluride, Maui, and Bucerias outside Puerto Vallarta; and cities across the country. The girls entered their teens. The man who drew circuit diagrams on Hawaii's beaches and worked long hours prototyping new inventions talked retirement. He never did wear a watch.

I remember no conversation, no deliberation about going to the British Virgin Islands, accepting the invitation to sail with another family, close friends, for two weeks. Like drops of water congealed in a wave, we were just going. You loved adventure; I always worried about something, this time the sailing prowess of our captain. Because we were going together, I put aside my worry, finding courage in your strength and happiness.

Between booking travel, getting the girls scuba-certified and you recertified, planning menus and buying gear, I carried on daily activity, suspending thoughts of the trip until we landed in the balmy St. Thomas airport. The ferry to Road Town, a beat-up, metal contraption decorated by chipped metal seats, got us there safely enough. Our dinner photo shows eleven already tanned, athletic people: two extended families with perfect smiles.

We knew it would not be a perfect vacation. Seventeen-year-old Ashley had become hostile, asserting, "None of my friends' moms worked. You left me with nannies. You weren't there for me." Her anger, mostly directed at me, encroached. I vowed to ignore as much as I could. I could see that she was hurting you, too; more than once you told me. Your sister who joined us for the first week offered to take her to Kansas. You told me you didn't want that, you wanted Ashley to come through this with her parents.

We found our boat in the harbor, our fifty-four footer. As designated dive master, you immediately became busy with ropes, tanks, buoyancy compensators, and wet suits. Simon, our captain, absorbed himself in navigation, radios, and controls. Sally and I took a cab to the market, an overcrowded jumble of people leaning against buildings, lingering in the parking lot. The inside overflowed with undersized carts pushing against each other through narrow aisles lined with food and beverage to satisfy a mix of nationalities. The produce was spotty; meat, cheese, and dairy safe enough as long as our boat had good refrigeration. We loaded up for a week.

The sign across the road warned: "Prevent the spread of HIV. Practice the ABC's. A = Abstinence B = Be faithful C = Condomize." The natives weren't overly friendly, or unfriendly. We were guests; this was their island.

Do you remember, the sun went behind clouds as we motored out of the harbor to open water, but it was still sticky hot? We sailed leisurely, Sally and Simon calling out the names of islands as we passed. There was a debate about making it to Foxy's, a well-known watering hole. A small, white crescent of sand took priority. We dropped anchor; some set off for the beach while you skiffed with others to a choppy dive spot at a rock outside the harbor. Our sand, white against azure water, bright under sun undisturbed by wispy clouds, held us warm. We dug holes with Sally's three-year-old. You came back.

Setting out again with purpose, we ditched Jost Van Dyke, home of Foxy's, and sailed fast to stake out our night's mooring at Cane Garden Bay. The three-year-old screamed in Sally's arms, "I hate this, I hate this. I want to go home." Sally tucked her between towels cradling her to sleep. You slipped your arm around me, laughing at my book, its pages whipped by wind.

You gaze at me now from the pictures. Lounging on deck, shirt open, hat low, calm water behind you, verdant hills rising from the edge of the distant shore.

Sitting at dinner between your older sister, Barbara, and Julia, chin lifted, smile crooked, the reflection of my flash in your glasses does not hide your happiness.

Dog paddling toward the boat in Cane Garden Bay, a squint at me on deck, you are saying something, likely, "Do you have my glasses?"

Back on deck, showering against a backdrop of ocean and islands receding one after the other in fading mists against a flat sky, you beam a smile.

Sailing took on a rhythm, a cadence of harbors, moorings, dives, snorkeling in caves, swimming to a near shore for drinks in bars that spanned tiny clearings between coconut palms. Pelicans skimmed the water and landed, teetering transients on buoys. Seagulls dogged us as we sailed, darting near and away, near and away again. Dolphins appeared, chattering, then slipped under our wake. We stopped at Cooper Island, where frangipani and tamarind trees were posted with signs: "Sea Grape Boutique" and "Sorry We Don't Accept Garbage." We stopped there more than once for its lounge chairs and long shallows lapping water onto the beach.

That was a good spot for the three-year-old, but not for Ashley. I told her we would both cut the trip short if she could not change her tone. The opportunity would come in a day or two when we landed to restock for the second week. She retorted, "You really want me to leave, Mom? NO." Though we were both hurt, you remained steady, "She needs love. She just needs our love."

Do you know, you were wrong—and right?

I hold you in my mind's eye strong against the mast, letting wind scatter your hair as you inhale salt, meet gentle spray. I relive dinners I smelled before eating. You barbequed, deck-side, making smoky rich tastes start at the back of my throat. With the fade of each day, darkness sealed us, particles in the sea, in earthscape after filtered sunsets, into night. Your look said it; you made those sunsets for me.

You kept your promise to the girls, and they loved every minute, each scuba diving in different and characteristic ways. Julia memorized tables, logged her dives immediately upon returning to deck, and commandeered a camera to record sea life. Ashley needed continuous reminding of the buddy system and refused a wet suit, preferring just a rash guard over her bikini. I relive the one post-dive conversation.

"Who throws garbage dumpsters into the ocean?" spoken indignantly by Sally in her clipped, British accent.

"Couldn't see anything and wondered why everyone was pointing in that direction," someone else said.

"When I found Ashley she was already inside." You were not happy that she once again had left the group.

"Daddy, I saw air masks hanging down and these baby turtles that were so new they weren't even tagged," Ashley said. "It was so cool."

You conceded that she led the group into the sunken plane, her prize: seeing its shy occupants before they could flee the divers.

We lingered in dark waters, dark skies on the Fourth of July. Fireworks spat their explosions, formations, and patterns dim in the distance over American islands. We were a country away, in shadow and blackness lit by stars. We sailed on.

Virgin Gorda's hillsides, boulders and harbors called us to hike, climb, and snorkel. At the Bitter End Yacht Club, bars appeared on my cell phone for the first time on the trip; we both rushed to call our office. You went first, only to flip the phone willy-nilly into the harbor. The group around you saw it happen and howled, anticipating my anger, your smile like a crack in glass when you told me about my phone. We didn't need to call the office.

These moments all happened, but what stays with me now: your arm slipping around me, the good-night-I'm-so-tired kisses, the here-I-am-coming-back-on-deck smiles of triumph. Oh, what I'd give for a smile of triumph.

Did I ever tell you? I don't think so. Many nights on our imperfect sail, as we folded into our berth like pages, side by side, long in our envelope together, I fell asleep thinking, "This just might be our honeymoon."

Meditation

January, 2008

It was the anniversary of your funeral, a day following a week of sadness, a season, and a year of sadness. We flew to Salt Lake City, my first trip with Ashley, who had not traveled until now; she said in a whisper that it felt wrong without you. She wanted to show me where wilderness transformed her.

As our plane banked into valley surrounded by mountains, I glanced out at the misty snow. In an instant, color started, a sunset where there had been only white over white, clouds over mountains—crimson, pink, and orange; electric against broken clouds; powerful brightness. Unutterably beautiful, the scene gripped me in a sudden breath, a gasp; I was struck again, remembering the day of your funeral when light flooded through stained glass windows at the side of the altar.

Ashley looked into the sunset and said, "Dad's here with us. I know it." I squeezed my hand around hers.

Sudden light at your funeral had spilled over us, in a moment through brilliant primary-colored, stained glass, twin depictions of the baby adored by Magi, and Martha learning at the feet of Jesus. The light found our family in the front pew before communion, lingering on us, noticed by others in the front of the church.

With one last squeeze to Ashley's hand, I gathered for our Utah landing, meeting our driver, and the short trip in descending light to a tiny resort interleaved between vertical showings of white: Sundance. We skimmed through a parking lot to register, taking in dark wood of the building outside, entering on a golden oak floor, pinewood reception desk and walls, interrupted by a giant river rock hearth, lightly reaching flames at its center. Back in our SUV, our driver picked his way through the night, turning and jogging on ever narrower roads, then we stopped. He guided us on a tiny path past one condo then another and another, each with shadowy entryways, doors within dwarfed by giant icicles. At the end of our path, he unlocked the door before us, turning on lights and depositing our luggage. We stepped into a living room with couches and well-stuffed chairs around a rock hearth. Our driver lit a fire as we explored bedrooms. This was home for three nights, our shelter within glowing paneled walls, oversized icicles now sentinels outside.

It was the place of a dream, a place you would love. The warmth, almost too hot, lacked for your touch, your laugh, your happy looking forward to the next day's skiing. I missed your "Sweetheart, let's get to bed early so we're on the slopes before everyone else." The bed was large, inviting, cold without you to wrap myself into. The heat unbearable, aching for you, I got up, fiddled with the thermostat, and got back in bed damp, again cold.

In this dream of a place, drivers answered our call, transporting us in silent hybrids to dine in a large room with tall, glass windows reaching as high as the peak of the vaulted, wood ceiling. Antique hand tools of every shape, size and imaginable purpose lined each quadrant of dark-paneled walls arranged in meticulous geometries as if like shapes had naturally found one another and agreed to stick together. We ate meals of trout, tortilla soup, salads sprinkled with corn and beans, and searched around for stars expected for the film festival but recognized none. Ashley ordered large waffles with whipped cream for breakfast. I sipped my tea, you rising in my heart as I thought of skiing just outside the door. We would have skied together.

Crossing over a snowy footbridge, we reached the ski shop and rented equipment. I insisted on helmets, remembering the first time you nearly died, expert skier though you were, pitching headfirst into a tree stump, fortunately hitting with your shoulder rather than your head. That made a believer out of you; we became a helmet family. On the ride up the chairlift my old sidekick, anxiety, kicked in, and I thought hard about wrapping my arm around Ashley's knowing that it was not your arm, and it would not give me the comfort of your strength. We sat, four skis dangling. The wind picked up. We reached the top, sliding off to a stop, choices before us—cat track down the slope we just ascended, another track to a bowl of slopes in the distance. We set off to explore one, then the others, in glimmery snow agitated by sudden gusts.

We pulled zippers to chins, wrapping into our parkas as the wind grew steadily stronger.

We pushed to the peak again and again, wind resisting our chair ride up a blustery slope: down, up again, down a different way then up and across to a warming hut, drank hot chocolate while looking out over valleys on either side of us. The lack of you, always an empty spot on the quad chair that we rode to the top, tore at me, my fear of height rising larger than my love of skiing. I didn't have your arm now, and felt lost in the air, safe on the ground. Wind ripped through us; we agreed, "Call it a day?"

At the bottom of the mountain, busses of afternoon snowboarders streamed in from Salt Lake City, loads of people we were happy to avoid. It felt right to rest in our cabin, warm, reflective in writing, cozy in naps until dinner among the tools, still no stars in sight. Our plans for a very early morning drew us to sleep, me dreaming, at first not remembering, then panicked. The alarm didn't sound in time. *We'll miss our driver, miss the meditation in Ashley's special place, the one she wants to show me. We will miss meditation because the alarm failed us. What time is it, time for the alarm? I set the alarm on my phone; the alarm hasn't sounded. It must not be time….*

A knock at the front door jolted me out of night's tossing and turning, still in the dream. Insistent knocking. I opened the door to our driver, yelled; we scrambled and rolled into the dark SUV. I sat next to a grey-haired man in tuxedo pants, his girth accentuated by a black down jacket. Our guide, of sorts; at least our driver.

You would have had a great hearty chuckle at the tumble into the SUV.

Snow blustered in the still dark morning, making me feel I had to stay awake, pay attention. I focused on the driver, the road.

"This snow is gonna get a lot thicker at the pass." He spoke in a tenor twang, the regional accent of a Provo son. Snow gusted, white, whipped thick like cream swirling as we blazed through high passes.

"Don't believe I caught your name," I said.

"Ron," the man of few words glanced sideways at me.

"I saw trout on the menu and wondered if it's local." Ron told me the trout was local and then of weekends with a buddy, fishing on nearby lakes, a tent pitched on ice.

Dawn came, early light cautious over a new terrain, the Castle Mountains. Teased by a sunrise that turned into a glare, we adjusted, thankful for daylight showing our way. Landscape flattened, low scrub pocked new snow's perfect spread in all directions. We drove on straight roads between flat fields toward a new stand of mountains in the east, Ashley asleep in the seat behind ours. Reaching the mountains, color crept ever darker into the landscape, brown showing through snow, reds, sienna, veins of green, a wash of green ore in the red, into Moab, high-desert wilderness.

I breathed in color, majesty, knowing with certainty why you returned here. We drove by entry points you passed through on your journeys to bike, camp and explore red monuments. As we passed, I longed to make the turn into the places you had been, to find you again by retracing your path along slippery rock, vistas, and precipices, to touch you. Images of you forging into bushes thick with hanging caterpillars, splashing into icy, mountain waterholes, hooting and hollering on a slide down a snowy slope, sitting at the edge of a cliff overlooking a pristine valley, or simply smelling every unique tree and plant that never asked for acknowledgement. I longed to go there, feeling you as I had in many other places that you loved, lingering, waiting for us to catch up. I will return.

I felt palpable curiosity from Ron, who told me most folks went north. I saw him wonder, finally speculating. "You're visiting a farm."

It came out of me in a voice I hardly recognized, mine. "My husband had cancer and died. During that time our daughter went here for help with some problems. She healed here."

The landscape before us turned white again. Moab behind us, we turned toward Colorado, more mountains, white fields on either side. We left the main road in a tiny town, turning at the flimsy highway marker called out in our directions. The man in tuxedo pants and I were newly partners, searching our way over unmarked snow cover for the right country road. This was a landscape of white against white; mountains in the distance, wisps for clouds mirroring the expanse of earth across a soft, blue sky, roads streaked with slush, shimmering white fields faintly yellow in the distance from sudden showings of winter wheat that I had never before seen. We turned and went straight, turning back to restart, then finding our direction over many miles, finally crossing a cattle gate, one signpost that our search was done to the next, a large teepee. We got out of the car. Ron stayed for a nap.

The sun hinted at warmth; cold stung us. Guides met us, hugging Ashley, then me, Ashley's family. They looked at our winter down wear and outfitted us with another layer, coats and overboots for warmth. We had missed the meditation, arriving just at the end, foiled by country roads. Pam, our host, was a therapist, savvy about hearts, a mender of souls. She turned to Ashley and asked, "What would you like to do?"

Stopped in a path surrounded by low juniper and high sage, Ashley answered with reverence, speaking the language of this place, "I'd like to do an 'I feel.'" She stopped as we gathered in a circle, facing one another; Pam picked it up, saying, "I feel so happy that you have chosen to come here and that you are doing well," turning to

Ashley who, again reverential, said, "I feel almost afraid, as if something might have changed, that it won't be as I remember it." They looked to me as pristine beauty around us newly pressed against my chest until I breathed deeply, pulling this place into the corners of my body and my heart. "I feel grateful to be here with Ashley, open to what we experience together," exhaled into crisp chill.

Turning away from the teepees close by, we passed a gateway of small flags hung on a wooden frame. Bright squares fluttered in the breeze, showing symbols, flags made by the hand of a careful author.

I found him, asked him to tell me the story of the symbols.

"There are five different colors: blue, yellow, red, green and white. The story depicted is for those who come here. It's Native American wisdom, our prayer for these kids. It's the horse prayer. No matter what the horse does, may its rider have the energy to maintain a straight, rider's posture."

We walked to a clearing, Ashley ahead of us, orienting herself within circles of juniper, sage and the placement of the camp. "This was my spot, my tarp and sleeping bag were here. This is where I looked up at the stars and saw the same stars you saw where you were. The stars were my comfort. Lily and Madison slept in that clearing and the one over there." Ashley showed us, gesturing, but spoke to herself. Pam led us to the camp where we met guides and two girls. They were girls with stories, not ours to tell, shared in the shelter of the teepee, with shy questions of Ashley about life and choices. "What was it like for you here?"

Ashley told me she identifies a person by their hands. "I got close to some of the girls. When anyone put out a hand, I recognized who it was. I knew everyone's hands. I went home, and Dad was sick. His strong, healthy hands were white, withered, and barely able to hold on with their former strength. I didn't recognize any of my family's hands. They were all different."

We sat still in the teepee, Ashley at the center, Pam listening and pacing us, feeling our way. She easily chuckled at the memory of quintessential defiance, Ashley insistent on keeping over a dozen pierces open in wilderness using twigs and spiral notebook wire. Ashley told me, "Pam talks with her eyes."

I spoke of the calm we have discovered together, the mornings Ashley sits opposite me starting homework on the couch across the room from the chair where I write. We naturally fall into a conversation, perhaps about Ashley's homework, perhaps about something else, a thoughtful exchange, a deepening closeness. As I spoke of this thing that happens, I said, "I have come to realize in those moments that there is nothing more important on earth than being there in that conversation with Ashley." Pam answered, "It's rare to have that with a nineteen-year-old. How does it feel to be here, Ashley?"

Ashley spoke slowly. "What I have been noticing since we got here is that time feels like it has stopped, and I felt that when I was here before. Time stopped for me, and the outside world became nearly a figment of my imagination: non-existent. I'm so happy to know time still stops here."

Cold started at the nose, reaching into throats, lungs, guts, butts, and toes as we sat sheltered from wind but without the benefit of movement. We rustled ourselves, standing, and emerged from the teepee to the campground. "I'd like to find you some shards." Snow cover thwarted Pam's search, and I wondered what shards she meant. "This land was inhabited by Indians who left pottery shards everywhere you look." Pam continued to poke around in the snow. Finally, she found one, then another and another, broken evidence of lives in this place long before ours. Where had they gone? Were they of the Ute tribe now living on nearby reservations, ancestors whose shards and souls remained with their land, their home?

We hiked a trail to a makeshift fence that Pam opened by twisting and releasing twisted hanger wire that held two loosely hinged gates together. We stepped across to a flat bluff, passing under a makeshift arch decorated with more flags. Primary colors, bearing symbols of the world's religions: Hinduism, Native American, the Sikh, Judaism, Buddhism, Islam, Christianity, and Daoism. In all, there were nine flags, jeweled colors against the white panorama: the ninth in the middle of the others, a globe of the world united its adjacent neighbors, Buddhism and Judaism, and by extension all the religions of humanity, the pureness of individual, human spirit.

"The medicine wheel is for special ceremonies; we treat this as a holy place."

Pam looked just past where we stood at a large circle roughly thirty feet in diameter fashioned out of rocks, pieces of wood, more pottery shards and several small animal skulls crowning rocks along the perimeter. At the center, a smaller circle of rocks formed a symbolic circle of fire, the heart of the larger whole, a celebration of the individual's life journey.

"Ashley, this is your time." Pam's stillness spread through me. I wondered what Ashley felt.

She seemed to be of this place, stepping slowly into the large circle close inside the perimeter rocks, walking the symbolic journey of life slowly, perhaps knowing her journey would continue to change. She walked the circumference with pause to reflect on objects forming the perimeter: skulls, stands of Mormon tea, pottery shards positioned on the rocks. Pam turned to me, "Now you join Ash at the circle." I stayed just outside the perimeter, making my way gingerly around, stopping at a quarter circle from where Ashley stood. Pam completed the ritual walk. We faced each other, each walking forward to the circle of fire, the medicine wheel's core.

"Ashley, you made your journey here, and you completed what you came here to do in this place. Be proud. Be strong. I'm going to step away now so you can be with your family."

Pam walked some distance outside the circle, leaving Ashley with me, in our minds including Julia, a newly constituted family, together now in a life no one could have expected. Goblet-shaped tears plopped from Ashley's eyes; she seemed to smile and then cry again.

"I'm so proud of you, Ashley, and Dad's proud of you, too. You know it. You can feel it, right?" She nodded, her tears subsiding some as she answered, "Yes, I do."

We hugged one another, breathed in the air, the moment, the accomplishment, the journey, together. Slowly, with a new reverence for the healing of this place, we made our way back to Pam.

"This land is all under the Bureau of Land Management now. It used to belong to the tribes and some of our guides have seen spirits out at the edge of the bluff, more than once." Pam explained as we retraced our steps back through the fence and the path. "I don't see spirits, but the folks who do have seen them near our medicine wheel."

And then the question. "How're you doing?" I felt her arm slip around mine, small antidote for the sudden tightness at my throat, the ache again dropping through me, the thought to take my time and breathe before trying to answer. "Are you back at work? Are you taking time for yourself?"

I breathed deep before each answer, shrugging my face into the high, zipped collar of my jacket, and got through it. Familiar answers to familiar questions, while we walked another landscape I had never seen, everything before me new, fresh, and cold.

Nearing the main teepee, we stopped again in the path, facing one another. "Let's take a moment together," Pam said. "I'll start by saying that I feel the rawness in your hearts. And I feel the good work you have done, the closeness of your family." She turned to Ashley.

"I feel so relieved that this place is the same, the land is the same, and that time still stops for people who come here."

Tightness in my throat, my mind was on you, Doug, our shared anguish at sending Ashley away, the anguish of losing her and then you. Chill air against my face brought me to the beautiful land around us, certain that you would have loved this place as Ashley did, and I now did, too: flooding sunlight, Ute Mountain in the distance imprinted on me as you welled up within me, love overwhelming.

"Doug is with us here. We love our girl and know this was a special place that changed our family. It meant so much to see the place and meet the people who reached into Ashley's great heart."

Just beyond us in the parking area, Ron brought himself into a chubby stretch, catlike, next to our black SUV, and then paced, his tuxedo stripes shimmering in the snowy lot. We stopped in teepees to return our borrowed layers and hugged Pam with many smiles and the shared satisfaction that humans had, with intention, traveled and come together to express love for one another. As we drove away, Ashley asked if she could go back next year.

We retraced our tracks over snowy roads grey with slush and falling light, soon leaving the flat expanse of fields, heading into the first stand of mountains before us. Nighttime fell as our SUV skimmed along roads between shadowy slopes. It was the ride of a dream, dark, certain, a comforting return on the same roads we traveled. Black night, fast changes in landscape, clear mountain passes, strip malls lighting the last valley before us and a turn to the mountain road that would take us in a dream to the icicle sentinels that we would leave in the morning.

We closed our eyes, feeling your powerful, ethereal hug, your smile washing over us, together always.

Understanding Moonseed

This was truly my mother's last journey. It started in the morning with her urn placed deep into my backpack. On top of the urn I added the polished mahogany box containing my dog Sunny's remains. Hoisting the whole heavy pack, I walked out of the hotel to rent a car.

At this point I heard my mother backpedaling, "Oh, you didn't have to go to the trouble. Anything you chose would be perfectly fine."

No excuses acceptable. I had a letter dated Sept. 15 1994, in which she outlined her plan to be buried with her parents in the Canby City Cemetery. The letter was heavily noted with her thoughts about a new granite marker including her name with theirs to be placed at the burial site. Her wishes could not have been more clear, though foreshadowing her dementia, she had misspelled her father's name.

Soon she was off my back, in the rear seat of a sleek black Volvo.

I had flown to Minneapolis knowing I would drive to Canby to bury my mother and my dog in what I regarded as my last act of care for my mother.

At first, I had a hard time with the thought of burying her so far from California, but it was my mother's wish to be laid to rest with her parents. Family though we are, we are not grave visitors by any stretch of the imagination. Peace came to me in a very simple plan. My mother loved our black lab, Sunny, who had died within days of her. There were times when she visited our house and, silent in dementia, stretched a hand taking up one black ear between thumb and forefinger, rubbing and humming to the dog. She was at our house, but visited only the dog. While she had lived in California for her last seven years, it made sense to place my mother according to her wishes in Canby, and to place Sunny with her there as an eternal reminder of her West Coast family.

On a crisp morning, the day after arriving in Minnesota, I got directions and left Minneapolis listening to Coltrane and wondering why every city I visit has better jazz radio than the Bay Area. At first my excitement was palpable. I had told myself this would be a pretty straightforward trip. By Eden Prairie, only about 30 minutes into my journey, I was short of breath, signaling my old sidekick, anxiety, rising in my stomach.

At the turnoff toward Shakopee/Chaska, white noise usurped Coltrane; I hit the radio's seek button in my rental. Jim Morrison turned up immediately, and I set a course for classic rock as long as I could get it.

It was clear that this drive was not going to be the California freeway experience I live. Nor would it be a Midwestern toll road experience. Four-lane roads quickly became two-lane county roads. I was alone for long stretches, unchallenged by a single car in either direction.

Crossing the Minnesota River for the first of several times through towns, population 1,323 or less, I slowed to the 30-mph speed limit. Gone was the notion that I'd drive the 164 miles in less than the four hours Mapquest advised; I understood why the time estimate was so long.

At the point where I was to turn left on Flying Cloud Drive, I messed up and had to backtrack on the highway, sudden tears blurring the road ahead.

Memories of my childhood took me to Chicago's State Street, eternally embarrassed by the ankle-high shoes my mother insisted I wear until I was around four. My mother had spent most of her life in Chicago, until I had moved her to California because of the worsening dementia. We stopped for a smiling exchange with Mrs. Emkie, a blue-haired lady my mother knew casually.

Talk, talk, talk. I started a series of tugs at the hand folded around mine. Mrs. Emkie noticed and said, "She's such a lovely girl, Margaret."

Simultaneously, I had tugged harder, tilting myself at an angle away from the conversation.

My mother relished comments like Mrs. Emkie's, taking them as a reflection on her. She flashed her most generous Hollywood smile, digging her fingernails into my hand to prolong the moment of appreciation.

I think she loved me until I got a mind of my own. She did her best; I know that. As a teenager, no longer little and cute, I argued every chance I got. She taught high school and surely understood something about teenagers. Sometimes I didn't come home, preferring to stay with friends in the suburbs. As a mother, I would have been beside myself and filed a missing person report. She didn't. Perhaps she trusted me. Perhaps she knew the days of controlling me with her fingernails were long gone. We shopped, went out for hamburgers, and she laughed at my running commentary on politics and people we knew. Although she had a life before me, she had made me a centerpiece of her life until I escaped.

As a result, I didn't begrudge the weight of her urn or the drive.

As the corn towered over each side of my car, I reflected on my single-mindedness about returning her to Canby. Canby is her place, not mine, but it holds some shadowy foundation for my origins. Driving that two-lane road, I was newly aware of my own passage into a place where I was in some way rooted, connected to people and lands I never knew. Their legacy formed me as surely as the people of those lands formed those before them in earlier years.

The rural road narrowed again and meandered. Verdant grassy ditches dropped at each side of the concrete. Cornfields stretched just feet away on either side. It felt like my car was lifted, floating on a sea of corn in every direction. I grabbed my camera, snapping a shot of stalks towering over the car on each side.

The sameness of the terrain meant that the only way I could know when to turn was by setting my odometer and paying close attention to sparsely marked county road signs. Lulled by the sea of vegetation and the road's gentle curves along the fields, I jolted to a stop realizing that I'd missed a turn by three miles. Doubling back, I reset the odometer and panicked when my turn didn't come up at the three-mile mark. I was out here in the middle of nowhere. Not a person, not a house in sight. If my turn didn't appear, I wondered if it would be better going on or going back? And where was the closest help? I imagined being stuck in the birth canal faced with the impossibility of turning back, waiting for the next push toward light. To my relief, my turn appeared on my left.

I was very close now. A road sign welcomed me to Yellow Medicine County, named for the bitter root of the Moonseed plant with its crescent-shaped seeds and narcotic flowers used by local Dakota and Sioux tribes for medicinal purposes. Toxic in the wrong hands, it had healing properties for a wide range of ailments. Tea made from the roots was used to treat indigestion, arthritis, bowel disorders and as a blood cleanser; the root itself was used on chronic sores.

I had visited this place forty years ago as a teenager and before that, as a child. Recognizing nothing, I continued to follow directions, setting the odometer at every turn. At last another sign welcomed me to Canby, home of the state's wrestling champions. I turned left on the main street and left again into the funeral home.

A young woman greeted me. "You must be Mary. I'm Toni."

Her beefy frame looked comfortable in jean shorts and a fifties sleeveless blouse. Her short hair was pinned babydoll style to one side. We sat down at a round pine table with country kitchen chairs to compare notes on granite color, engraving, and floral decorations in the corners of a new grave marker. I asked if she knew the family that had purchased the farm my family had owned until twenty years ago. She brought out a phone book the size of a thin paperback novel. Each section listed the names of people in a single tiny town, ten towns in all. I found the name and address, and asked for directions. I wanted to return to Minneapolis by dinnertime, but just maybe I'd drive by.

Toni accepted my check and stood up. "We might be able to get this installed before the first snow. We'll send you a picture. I'll take you to the cemetery now."

I followed her Suburban onto the main road through town. Old brick buildings along the main drag offered up one theater, an Ace hardware, a health and yoga studio, and some other small stores. A wide-windowed diner that Toni recommended for lunch stood opposite a millworks and lumber yard. We drove on, soon arriving at a cemetery flanking both sides of the road.

Toni turned left, and I followed, stopping behind her at the side of the dirt path. Many tombstones bore the family name, but Toni led me on foot to a spot in the middle of the cemetery where a hole awaited. I looked around at the sparkling granite garden, and then down.

"There's no marker!"

"No, but they probably had one when they died. It was so long ago it was probably something made of wood."

How do you know who is in which spot? I wondered.

"We had to go in sideways to find the exact placement of the coffins," she continued. "Your mother will actually be between her parents."

I gazed down at the square pit at my feet.

"It was the custom in their day that in north-south facing cemeteries the husband was buried on the north side of his wife. To protect her from the north wind, it was said. So your grandfather would be here and your grandmother would be there on the other side of where your mother will lie."

We both eyed the spots where my grandparents lay beneath the grass.

"I'll leave you then. About half an hour you need? I'll tell them to come finish up."

I thanked her and turned back to my car to retrieve the urn and the box. One in each arm, I returned to the hole, first placing the urn and then the box. They looked very small. There they were. My mother and my dog, at rest at last. I looked to each side of the open hole. This was the closest I would ever come to my grandparents.

"My grandparents." Foreign and wonderful words. A concept made real in a cemetery. I had grandparents. And for that matter all these distant cousins – blood relatives under those granite tributes.

My grandparents would finally share a granite marker with my mother.

I went back to the car for my camera.

I will never come here again.

This is their place not mine.

I snapped pictures of the urn and box in their resting place, several small monuments bearing the family name, relatives, and a wider angle of the cemetery. That's all I needed.

I turned away but after a moment turned back again imagining the north wind, the banks and drifts of snow, spring rains on fledgling corn stalks, forebears more than a century ago erecting barns, pounding timbers to form houses, and before them, the people who lived on these lands and cared for it as their own – before our Scandinavian families settled here, the generations of native peoples who coexisted, hunted, farmed, and fashioned their life against harsh elements.

Where are their bones, their markers, the places where their legacy can be honored by modern generations?

My heart filled with all these images, newly connected to this land and the generations of people who made a home here, made a home in my imagination and heart.

As I returned to the car, I could hear my mother again. "Oh c'mon. We've driven all this way. You might as well just look at our farm and take a picture."

I turned left on the main road in the direction I'd been told. Six more miles. I had the time.

At the hilltop Toni described, I turned right on the small county road and began marking the dirt road "streets" that materialized exactly every mile. I found the one and turned.

"First place on the left," Toni had said. The name on the mailbox was right, but it was not the farm I remembered clearly from pictures and seeing it as a child. A man on a tractor worked empty land alongside a gravel drive lined with cars that led to a mobile home.

I looked down the road at the next farm. That could have been the one. Lush trees surrounded what I remembered as the white frame two-story Victorian house that I had seen but never been in. I envisioned the chicken coop across from the house, behind that a barn and silo. Had they subdivided the farmland to make a homestead for this young couple? I did not drive on to look closer.

This was their place now. I said goodbye to all of it – to the legacy of that land and earlier generations, to family that had never been mine – and turned back through town, retracing my route to this remote place, resolute that my place, my peace, were to be found elsewhere.

About the Dreams

My therapist was a boat refugee.

A long time ago, I spent nine years in Jungian therapy with a wise and scholarly seer. He told me: when women from the East coast dream of an assault, the attacker is Black or Puerto Rican. Women on the West Coast swap in a Mexican.

My nightmares are not about assaults, but instead imagine a walk through Chicago's Cabrini Green on West Division Street as it was in the '70s, several miles immediately west of where I grew up on East Division Street. I never did have to take that walk.

Like my dreams about lighting a cigarette without restarting a habit, I interpret the Cabrini dream as a walk into a danger zone—a psychic warning about my waking life.

As a six-year-old, I knew about gangs.

From my earliest awareness, my mother, Margaret Geneva Peterson, taught in the roughest public schools on the South Side of Chicago—Marshall and Crane. They were legendary for their gangs, which I would not have known, except that she filled my six-year-old-year ears with stories of teachers being slashed and stuffed in student lockers in her school.

I was afraid for my mother's safety, even as she hissed about men who fathered children and left them to be welfare dependents.

I was afraid, knowing she crossed picket lines of striking teachers, insisting that even the toughest of her Black students was entitled to public school education.

The Chicago police called it a gang encounter.

One cool summer night in 1971, I left my mother's apartment at 4 a.m., barefooted in jeans and a sweater. In my college angst, I walked for a bit, then turned back into the entry area of the apartment building. I didn't have a key.

For a moment I wondered if I should ring the doorbell and awaken my mother. The outer door opened. A young Black man stood before me. "Let's go for a walk."

Beneath his sweater was what could have been a gun. "Don't mess with me. You know the Black P Stone Nation? That's my gang. This is my gun. Let's go to the beach."

Oak Street Beach was a couple dark blocks away and once there, I was unfindable even if I screamed.

The Drake Hotel was half a block away on Michigan Avenue.

I walked at gunpoint to the corner, asking questions.

"I don't know about the Black P Stone Nation."

"You know about the Panthers? We're gettin' bigger."

"You work near here?"

"The Knickerbocker." The hotel opposite the Drake.

A part of me thought the gun was his forefinger, and that he was an off-duty parking garage attendant.

Another part of me thought I don't know enough to say it's not a gun. He was muscular and had his mind set on moving me to the beach.

The only certainty: I would be raped if I didn't get away.

At the corner after, "It's too cold…" and "It's too late…," he ran out of patience and punched me. I felt my eye immediately sting, swell, and tear up.

He grabbed the V of my sweater. I backed out of it. He punched me again, catching my shoulder as I ran the half block in my bra and jeans to the Drake Hotel, where I wrapped myself in a construction drape.

Apparently, I had screamed loudly enough before running to awaken the second-floor neighbors who called the police, as did Drake security.

At the hospital, the Chicago cop told me to stay far away from guys in gangs. He looked me over, flashed a fat wad of hundreds and, leaning over, confided to my breasts that he was "on the right side of things."

The cop was disgusting. So was the disgusting off-duty parking attendant with the fake gun under his t-shirt. They were in the same game.

I have never dreamt of that moment.

I arrived in San Jose, California over forty years ago with Chicago as base rock, a cautious, white girl. I knew nothing about Mexicans. I had moved west but still dreamed of having to walk through the west side of Chicago.

My Cuban therapist was brown. And definitely smart about me.

What is the color of living?

My vital, athletic husband died in 2007 after a short fight with cancer, leaving two teenagers and me. White people brought so many flowers that I called a nun to take some to the elderly nuns in the convent. White people brought chicken breasts and prayers.

My Peruvian housekeeper, Maria, told me to get dressed. I thought I was dressed in my late husband's clothes. Maria's first husband was gunned down when she was twenty-five and already had three small children.

Our Mexican gardener, Cris, showed up at the house to check the sprinklers. His crew showed up, one by one, to find a lost tool, to finish planting the hearty Mexican sage, and even to clean the gutters after an unseasonal rain.

Can we ever get it right, can we just keep trying?

I taught poetry some years ago to a small group of Latino boys at a local charter school.

They had been remedial learners, but were college bound. I brought in a new concept each of nine weeks. Simile, metaphor, rhythm, phrasing, etc. Thirty minutes on the concept with examples, forty-five minutes writing to a prompt, if possible, using the concept in their work. And forty-five minutes reading to each other what they had written.

We met around a table that was three feet in circumference. Six big guys and me with my laptop.

Somehow, we all found a space for the page on which we would write. And when they read, we all leaned into a space that was even smaller, as if we shared a secret.

A midair moment of Michael Jordan at the basket. A powerful bear that crusaded through a series of fables to fight social injustice. JFK was even mentioned forty years after his death—decades before these boys were born. They congratulated each other softly on having given voice to their own poverty, hunger, the gangs around them, their breaking families, and the dreams they had put into words.

"I wrote a song about that…Hey, it's got rhythm *and* repetition!"

"Wow man, that's a fable!"

"You really gotta a thing about…"

"Yeah, Obama is all that."

In our final afternoon, we assembled the best of what they had written into a collection, the school's first lit mag, *Nostra Verdad.*

Our Truth.

I'm sixty-six in a political environment that newly trends against public charter schools like the one where I taught—and thus unexplainably against a place of opportunity that surpasses national records for graduates in this population who succeed, progress to and complete college.

Every young person is entitled to education. That is the dream I share with my mother.

Journey of the Heart

I smelled the leather, cologne and antiseptic as the stethoscope pressed onto my chest, first in the middle, then on each side.

1958.

I scanned framed photos I'd seen before: the tall, balding, mustached and middle-heavy doctor standing beside rhinos, zebras, and elephants he'd shot in Africa.

That day, he heard something new in my five-year-old heart.

"When did this happen?"

My mother started forward on the leather bench, without answers. From then on, I was excused from gym and swim lessons due to a "heart condition." In college, a flu virus lodged in my heart, landing me a three-month hospitalization.

Yet I played tennis, hiked, cross-country and downhill skied. I fell in love and stopped smoking. My active life saved me. New doctors told me that I'd eventually need a valve replacement.

Occasionally my heart would trill inside my chest, an electrical problem that brought to mind the word "insufficiency"—the breath I could not hold onto.

After one quasi-breathless year, I asked Doug to accompany me to my cardiologist to ask when I would need surgery.

"Likely in five to ten years."

In the years that followed, leaking blood whispered to me as I came out of sleep. I had echocardiograms several times every year. I learned the dangers of ripped chordae, increasing pulmonary artery pressure and diminished oxygenation. I researched surgical techniques and hospitals, studied valve repair, the new norm. Instead of sawing through eleven inches of sternum to gain access to the heart, the procedure could be done through four small incisions at the side of the chest, using tiny, surgical instruments at the end of robotic arms. Time and science were on my side.

My heart was doing what it was supposed to until a detour. Rather than shutting tightly, my mitral valve fluttered open, allowing oxygenated blood to leak back rather than flow to the contracting left ventricle that would push the blood into the aorta. It was the cardiac equivalent of shoveling sand out of a pit where a portion of each shovelful simply falls backward, working harder to produce a lesser result. Over the years, the heart muscle enlarged.

After treating me for twenty-five years, my cardiologist heard something different. "That's really loud. The sound has changed. Let's get an echo."

Inconclusive results. "Your pulmonary pressure is up."

An overly tall man, his long frame folded and looped onto a tiny stool. He scoured through notes from prior years.

"Your pulmonary pressure was up three years ago and went down, so I guess nothing is materially different."

I was having more and more "bad days," awakening breathless, running out of breath climbing hills. While science and fitness had worked in my favor, I knew surgery was inevitable.

The new echo revealed torn chordae tendineae, the behind-the-scenes guide wires helping to open and close the valve during the normal cardiac cycle. Looking at prior echocardiograms, the chordae had been tearing since January, further increasing the risk for atrial fibrillation, stroke, and congestive heart failure. Putting his stethoscope down, my cardiologist concluded. "We need to think about getting this fixed."

It was a long appointment comparing my echocardiograms. "You may want to think about…" a week earlier had become "We need to…"

"You can do this anytime now. I'll make the call."

My time had come. All my research had given me a fragile confidence that I would live through the operation, undoubtedly with pain and weakness as I recovered, and that my life would be improved by having a heart that functioned normally.

*   *   *

"Mom, when did this happen?" Nineteen-year-old Ashley sat erect on the couch, her torso supporting a long neck, her large, blue eyes crowned by cropped platinum hair. "When did this happen, and why didn't you tell me?"

"I'm telling you when I have all the facts."

Her sister, next to her, drew her knees into her chest slouching, hugging her shins. She had green eyes like mine, widened as if to bore into all that I knew before I said it.

"You know how we'd go to the mall and suddenly I'd get weary and grumpy and didn't want to be there?"

Their heads nodded. Then I said, "You guys have known that there was a problem with my heart."

Julia's face went blank, awaiting the full explanation; Ashley started talking— too fast, insistent.

"Mom, this is terrible. You're going to have to be on immuno-suppressant drugs for life, aren't you?" Completely taken by surprise, I suppressed a laugh.

"No, Ashley, I'm not."

"We just studied this in bio. Anytime they put something in your body you run the risk of rejecting it. Yes, you are!"

"No, I'm not Ashley. Please stop interrupting and let me finish."

"You ARE!"

"NO, I am not."

She stood up abruptly, at five foot eleven towering over me for a moment before flouncing into the kitchen. "I can't believe you didn't tell me about this until now."

She kept up a muttered commentary that I tuned out as I turned to Julia. "She needs to let me finish what I have to say."

"No kidding." Julia's muscles tightened from her shoulders to her jawline. "She needs to just listen."

Julia needed to hear the research, the plan, and the prognosis.

A few minutes later, Ashley returned and resumed her upright pose. I picked up my narrative concluding with, "I see no reason for you girls to come to the hospital until I'm out of ICU. Mary will text you every report."

"No way. Mom. I'll come up right after my Wednesday morning class. The surgery should be well underway." I had known what to expect from Ashley. After swinging between denial and desperation before the finality of Doug's passing, she now needed to know every little thing and stay close, assuring herself that I would live.

"I'll come up after cross-country on Thursday." Julia said.

By this time I had researched and chosen my surgeon. I had put in place a support network for myself and the girls. Mary, our friend of thirty years, had been with me through the research, the doctor's appointments, the scheduling, the planning. She would be with me through the surgery, recovery, and afterwards at home. Doug's sister, Barbara, would stay with the girls. I had written the email to send to friends as the news spread. Mary and Ashley were contacts for information. I had written and sealed a note to be opened only if something went wrong. Mary was the keeper of that note, which contained details of my will and the final instruction: "Kiss the girls often and remind them that Doug and I love them forever."

I was ready.

I looked at my girls, knowing in my heart how they would agonize.

"You've been through so much. I'm so sorry to put you through this. It isn't cancer. This will be nothing like dad's illness."

Julia nodded; Ashley's eyes could not have been wider.

"There are three things you should know. One, there is every reason to believe they will be completely successful in repairing my heart valve. Two, I have done my homework and feel really good about both the doctor and the hospital, and three, you are going to meet the surgeon before any of this happens. So, you can think about what I've told you and ask anything you would like."

I looked at Ashley. Her voice was firm and insistent. Her eyes were something else, in motion and searching.

"I want to know if you're going to be on immunosuppressant drugs."

*   *   *

I went for an angiogram to determine if my coronary arteries had blockage that would rule out a "small incision" surgery. A nurse greeted me at the Cardio-Cath Lab.

"We've been waiting for you!" She shook my hand and handed me a clipboard.

A sour-faced woman appeared and scrutinized me. I unfolded my arms and offered my insurance card. "I bet you want this."

She ran off with it like a greedy scavenger but reappeared a minute later. "I need your driver's license, too."

"Come this way please, darling." The nurse's badge read Pilar.

She made the rounds; blood in a thin tube to a small container, IV, temp, cardio connections to the monitor, and blood pressure. Two new faces introduced themselves as the prep team.

Everything was routine, right through something inserted through the groin into the heart to see if its arterial superhighways were blocked.

The black-and-white screen displayed two branches stretched like roots of a tree against a grey shadow, wider at the top and narrower as they dropped. I watched dye run through these roots around a soupy, grey image—my heart.

My coronary arteries were not blocked. The procedure team rolled me back to Pilar, who checked my vitals.

"What does Pilar mean?"

"It's a Spanish name, but I don't think it means anything."

I listed some of the cultural names I remembered: "Aiyana"—Native American for eternal blossom.

"You know, I love my daughter's name, Amee, Spanish for "friend.""

"How old is she?"

"Thirteen, but I have two older ones, too. I've been through the teens."

I said, "Mine are both teenagers—two great girls with the sadness that we lost their dad, my husband, a year-and-a-half ago."

"Oh, no. How?" Pilar stopped at my side, looking into my eyes.

"Pancreatic cancer. Our younger girl was fifteen; our older seventeen."

Pilar looked at me. "You're beautiful, and so strong."

I wondered again if people consoled themselves by telling me I was strong. Her voice was strong, but with a softness that comes after years of sadness. Mine cracked often as I spoke.

Pilar continued. "I lost my husband, too. He was twenty-six. We had two children. We lived in Mexico City, but he was in California. I came here to be with him. After he died, I went back, suddenly a widow. Nobody looked at you the same. It wasn't a good place to be. Everything was there for me; I had it all. But there was nothing for the future. We moved back here."

I thought about the strength it took to move, support a young family, and get a nursing degree.

"You're strong. You'll find a good man. They're out there. You're too beautiful to grow old alone."

I found her prediction both comforting and enormous. Her message was about learning to make changes, not just accepting them, holding life sacred and with it, faith in new possibility.

I gave her the name Pilar: the messenger.

*   *   *

I walked from dark morning into the soft glare of can lights in the empty lobby, toward the elevator, through doors that closed with a shush as I pushed two. I followed the signs to the Short Stay Area where I was greeted, gowned, weighed, ushered to my second Betadine shower in eight hours, and re-gowned. False courage and mounting fear rose in my throat.

You can know something is coming for a long time and still dread it. The day had come. Doug was not there to take my hand in his, lean over, and whisper, "Keep up your positive energy. You need it now. Everything will be all right."

His sister Barbara, and Mary moved to my side.

We had been told that the easiest operations are taken first. I recognized the patient across the corridor from pre-op the day before. He smiled and nodded, looking like he was preparing to skipper a KrisKraft in the bay. Every feature in his wife's face twitched vigorously. The lighting shone dingy yellow.

A nurse with a wide smile stopped by looking crisp and in charge in navy scrubs. I liked her immediately. Next the anesthesiologist, an unpronounceable name, came to my gurney, looking well-scrubbed and too young, like her mommy dressed her and dropped her off at the hospital, adjusting her funny cap before sending her out the car door. She may have been slight and young, but her dark eyes held mine as I teared up and said, "Take good care of me."

My girls need to see a parent come through went through my head.

The three of us—Mary, Barbara, and I—looked at the clock. The guy across the corridor was gone, his twitching wife gone, too. Under yellow light, nurses and transport personnel hovered around the station—more people to give care as more people needing care checked in.

A cheerful guy introduced himself and rolled me through pushbutton double-wide doors down a blue corridor turning past steel equipment. We stopped at another doorway. Through the glass panes I saw a bright glow, the insistent, pulsating white light of the operating room. We waited through some confusion as people circled me talking on radios. I withdrew into my thoughts, eyes closed, tearing up. Then at my side a navy shadow rubbed my arm and said, "We know about your husband and your daughters. We'll all take very good care of you."

With that we were both in motion, rolling the next short distance into the operating room. I helped the nurses center me on the new gurney. I lifted my head, hearing a loud plastic ripping sound and found its direction to the left. "Someone just opened that big package," explained a voice.

Before lying down again, something caught my eye on the right, a Rube Goldberg of a thing with steel tubing and chambers, all surprisingly low to the ground. It dawned on me that this was the heart-lung machine that would sustain me, doctors at its controls exchanging carbon dioxide-filled blood for oxygen-enriched blood, keeping me alive as long as my heart was stopped.

The anesthesiologist was all business at my head, the doctor in charge directing the personnel around her, a second-string quarterback to the surgeon who was presumably closing up the captain somewhere down the corridor. "I'm going to give you something to take the edge off."

I looked up at a tiny bag on the IV pole, and then at the clock on the wall opposite where I lay. It was 8:50.

*　　　*　　　*

What a temple we have in each of us–tiny yet complete with atria and separate, well-sealed chambers, regulated by valves, a behind-the-scenes network of pulley cords that hold the valves tight, and superhighways that sometimes clog, honorifically named "the coronaries." The valves open and close in lockstep rhythm, regulating traffic, admitting only the visitors that belong in each chamber at each moment. The work of molecules is moment by moment in this tiny edifice at our core, a pumping station, the central hub of humanity, the heart.

Our hub beats 4,000 times an hour, 100,000 times each day, over 3.5 billion beats in a lifetime. At about eleven ounces, it is slightly larger than a fist. Each heartbeat pumps half a cup of blood through the entire cardiovascular system–62,000 miles of veins, arteries, and capillaries – in twenty minutes. Traveling at 38,000 miles per hour, our fastest interstellar spacecraft, Voyager 1, has yet to come close to the speed of blood.

What is the exact anatomical location of "having a lot of heart," "heart and soul," "taking heart" or "a heart of gold?" Is "from bottom of the heart" located at the descending thoracic aorta? Does "heartache" course through arteries and veins? Should "big-hearted" people get examined quickly? Enlarged chambers pose risk, though they can house many busy oxygen-rich visitors.

There are always visitors on a life-giving mission in this heart of ours. Blood rushes in on its errand of exchanging molecules filled with carbon dioxide for molecules filled with oxygen. The busybody mass of molecules carry out their mission with the help of squeezing atria, ventricles and regulatory valves. One can listen in on the rush from chamber to chamber, the noisy slosh-push that was, before echocardiography, described as lub-dub. The busybodies do their jobs pushed, squeezed, stopping and then rushing, all beyond the speed of space travel, their acceleration giving us each fresh breath of air and an oxygenated brain that can think clearly.

It makes sense that issues require that we get to the heart of the matter as the critical threshold for understanding. It's a lovely detail that lettuce, celery and artichokes all have hearts signifying the most tender essence of the vegetable before us.

We "pour our heart out" in our stories, we "put our heart" into an endeavor as a commitment, we "give it all our heart" as we strive for something, we give "blessings from the heart," and we hope to "win a heart." I suffer from a "broken heart"—the sadness that coursed through my body during and after Doug's death.

Heart pervades our symbolism, our stories, our myths, and our prayers—ever at the center of our language, our expression—ever the core of life.

*   *   *

My eyes fluttered open, resting on the clock. 9:00—different light. I must have drifted for a few moments. I blinked, summoning resolve for the next wave of sleep and the surgery. Sleep didn't come; I felt knives in my side and back.

"Your surgery went well, and you are just waking up." I heard the voice in motion at my side.

"I'm alive," I thought. "It's time for the next stage."

I thought of this surgery in phases: summoning the courage to walk into the pre-op area, entrusting myself to the care of other hands. Now the part I dreaded the most: waking up intubated. As I awakened more, there was less air. It came into my lungs as if through a straw. Perhaps you need less oxygen when you're in a drugged sleep. I was very wide awake, a package of anxiety and discomfort from things stuck in me: the plastic tube in my mouth, something in my back, in my shoulder blade, something that crossed my ribs into my chest. The tubes I didn't yet understand were hell.

I made a sound that I hoped was commanding and pointed to my mouth.

A face stopped in front of mine—dark eyes, round checks, large teeth and wild hair defying a ponytail. "My name is Joyce. I'm your ICU nurse. You have a breathing tube."

Nothing like stating the obvious.

"The breathing tube will remain until your lung inflates. You had a collapsed lung."

That was big news. Nothing I read about in any of my research. A complication? I remembered that my mother had a collapsed lung when I was young. That kept her in the hospital for weeks.

I pushed my hands up out of the sheets, one in the position of a pen and the other a pad of paper. Could I write what I wanted to say?

"Yes, the breathing tube will have to be there a while longer until your lung re-inflates."

Joyce defeated my hands with a sheet. The things crisscrossing inside me hurt, and I was very thirsty. Anxiety and pain seemed to require more air than I was getting. I closed my eyes and conjured Doug.

"Just rest now. Let your body have some time to get over the shock and start to heal," his voice calming inside my head. For a moment I wondered if I might sleep again. Something stabbed me inside my shoulder blade. I pressed my shoulder back into the pillow.

Resigned to being awake, I looked around. There were tubes everywhere.

Over the next thirty-six hours, the breathing tube came out, and the thirst got worse. I negotiated for water. "I'll get you some ice chips in ten minutes, but first I have to…"

Whatever it was took thirty minutes. Just when I thought she'd forgotten, she spooned a measly piece of ice into my cheek. I wanted to chew it but held the crushed lump in my mouth to melt. Evoking loaves and fishes multiplying, I sucked gingerly.

Over the next thirty-six hours, I negotiated for more ice chips. Blood was drawn every few hours from a network of lines stuck into my neck. Before and after each draw, saline was pushed into the lines to keep them open. I saw more of Joyce as she scrutinized me. The monitor produced the steady rhythm of my own heart. The cuff on my arm automatically inflated, yielding another measurement that Joyce dashed to record. I consumed a cocktail of intravenous meds, something called Lasix that sounded like it should eliminate facial wrinkles. The stabbing continued, and I negotiated a different position for my pillow. I heard the words "albumin" and "dopamine." Someone asked me how I was feeling. I saw a bag of blood attached above, my third I'm told. I knew my blood pressure was seventy-two over thirty-seven and remembered when Doug's blood pressure dropped that low, landing him in intensive care for treatment of infections. He got three tubes in his chest for weeks. One day with two, and I was in agony. He didn't complain. Someone asked how I felt? I felt fine. I knew I'd live and be healthy. More dopamine. More negotiation. 4 a.m., day two. Here's the scale. I stand for the first time. Retaining fluids says the scale.

Day two, my blood pressure stabilized. Having mastered Jello in every color and graduated to water from a straw, I settled into a nearby chair for a taste of lukewarm oatmeal. This was living. I got to complain about the food.

A new team took over. More blood draws, x-rays to measure the collapse, and suddenly I was sprung to a new unit, drainage tubes and all, still watching the clock.

*   *   *

In the days following surgery, the drainage tubes came out. I scripted my own entry and exit from the bed. Free of stabbing pain, I walked with hospital-level abandon. My breath short, my lungs still fighting fluid, I blew into a device and coughed, a textbook case.

Someone listened to my heart every four hours. "I wonder what it sounds like," I said to anyone with a stethoscope.

"Listen for yourself," a nurse finally said. I plugged the ends into my ears and heard two sounds, generic without the shushing that I had come to know as my heart. For a moment I felt sad, as if I had lost an old friend.

On day five, I left the hospital and rode home in Mary's car, lightheaded, grateful for sun, late summer and the sight of my house.

Mary worried out loud about "cardiac depression." I looked sideways in the car at the defined lines at the corners of brown eyes, knowing the smile that started at one corner would spread up her mouth to finish at the other eye. She was maid of honor when Doug and I married. She said she was honored to be my chosen pal through this. She mentioned cardiac depression a second time. I said, "I think it's a normal reaction."

I was sad, missing Doug. With my drainage tubes and drops in blood pressure, I got firsthand experience that he endured on a larger magnitude. He never complained; he just hoped to live. I complained, knowing I would live.

I was the woman with the broken heart, a heart that had been surgically repaired. My scars are the indelible marks of a happy life, a dim gash from hip to hip through which two children entered this world, and a swollen smile mirroring the curve of one breast lifted in love, tugged at for sustenance, opened to reshape my heart. The irony was not wasted on me. I had entered another season of healing.

*   *   *

Mary set our agenda, lots of rest and one day: the Monterey Bay Aquarium. We paused at the sea otters, moving on to the inner bay, through the circling sardines to the outer bay world. The white shark drifted past, both of us secure behind our fifteen inches of glass. I waited, still and hopeful. Fish glided by. One ray, then another, came closer. They opened white underbellies against the glass where they paused, ghostly beauties, each with a unique face and wing movements. I felt grateful, but held myself still, searching the back of the tank for another mysterious creature.

As if my concentration paid off, the water moved in a broad shadow: the shark again, slipping then darting forward. I settled my focus into the murk and found another large shadow. It moved back and forth, swaying and lingering, lifting and hovering, dropping and shimmering. The teasing thing came forward—a dinosaur-age, wearied surface, an anomaly of a fish, all head and tail. This beloved freak of a thing dives to 500 feet for a diet of crustaceans and eel, and then warms itself on the surface, sun-grazing on jellyfish while other creatures clean it. Weighing up to several tons, the sunfish is a surface hazard to boats, reminding all who encounter it of the unexpected.

I studied its texture, its painted monochrome lips framing a beaklike mouth, too small for the fish it must eat. It passed the glass with a cataract gaze and retreated, again a shadow and then an illusion.

Mary and I moved outdoors. "Let's not leave without doing the 17-Mile Drive, OK?"

Shortly, we were on Pebble Beach, avoiding bicycles, estimating the price of houses for sale, and admiring the ocean on our right. Suddenly before us a whale spouted and a second one sent up its plume. We drove past shoreline rocks and found the whales again.

Mary guided us through Pebble Beach to the oceanside highway and home. I was sleepy, quiet, and filled with the day. We passed artichoke fields nearing their season, dreamy in the mist of irrigation. We wound between hills dotted with cattle dwarfed by the expanse. The light softened as the sun set behind us. We entered the eucalyptus stand that marked the transition from coastal highway to Gilroy and the valley beyond, a grove where ragged giants make mystery of light filtered through blue-green, banana-shaped leaves drooping like spirits over all who pass. At the end of the grove in a strangely bright sky hung an oversized moon, luminous and full.

Going Back

We flew over mountains to flat lands, a patchwork of brown, mottled grey, green, and dusted white. Every so often a dotting house, barn, and silo denoted a human family ordering the landscape below us. The Midwest. I was born there. My seventeen-year-old, Julia, napped against my shoulder.

As we flew, I thought about the last times I went back, once to uproot my mother, whose withered mind needed the safety of care near our home in California. After that, I returned twice to place ashes in their designated spot. On the first trip, Doug and I landed and then drove north to a cemetery in Wisconsin to place his father's urn into the earth next to his mother's coffin. I took pictures as we sat there remembering his parents, newly aware that he was now the patriarch of the family. Two years later, I again transported an urn of ashes—my mother's—to take their place among the graves of a family I had only known through stories. I took pictures, knowing I would never go back to that place.

Years before all that happened, I had visited Puerto Rico, where under roiling clouds I walked to an oceanside cemetery situated between tenements. On a site fit for a Four Seasons resort, elaborate statuary marked the resting place of entire families. I thought to myself, "This is the most expensive place to bury the dead, a real estate tribute."

Now, I was back to my own roots. I drove into town passing the hospital where I was born and Rockefeller Chapel where I was baptized in a ceremony now memorable only because of a faded photo. Julia and I were on a college tour, so I advertised the route as "seeing the University of Chicago."

Julia said, "Impressive."

We drove into town after a day at the University of Michigan, where she had simply said, "I don't see myself here."

The next day, we would tour Northwestern, a campus I once called home. I fell in love there and started my life in the way one who has come into a certain age makes decisions that will define a future. We were young, too young for much more than graduation and cohabitation, which we did together for ten years before marrying. Along the way we moved across country, bought and sold houses and cars, started businesses, finally married and started a family. Our parents joined us in California and lived nearby, increasingly accepting our care. They died and we cared for their urns. My college sweetheart fought and then succumbed to disease, leaving two daughters and me to go on.

I had planned this winter trip to show our daughter another campus on her list of potential colleges and expose her to Chicago's chill.

Julia and I had driven from Ann Arbor in a misty winter skimming the ground between stands of leafless branches bunched together in flat expanses, stark land divided by crooked lengths of fence, silvery ponds and the occasional house and barn. I marked the milestones and memories of our route from car capital to the cereal capital of the country, then Kalamazoo—a city name that sounds like its own funky anthem—and a lakeside resort that brought to mind a photo with my mother on a boat—the photo more real than any memory of that childhood vacation. We rounded the southern tip of Lake Michigan, passing sand dunes I had never visited—no less vivid in my imagination—then into Gary, Indiana. I opened my window, sniffing the air for a stench I knew well, one belched from smokestacks crowned by flames, brilliant and defined as they reached skyward. The smokestacks remained, barely discernable shadows in the night. Something familiar found its way through my nose to the back of my throat. I wasn't sure if it was a lingering trace of industry or the imprint of memory.

We turned off on Garfield, passed through the University of Chicago and turned north on Lake Shore Drive, jogging onto the Outer Drive, which put us next to a black lake that was indistinguishable from a black sky. I was curious and a bit exhilarated to be returning to a place so filled with memories. I narrated: the Museum of Science and Industry, the Field Museum, Aquarium, and a renovated Soldier Field that I didn't recognize, Grant Park where I attended concerts and a recently elected president accepted the nation's call to leadership. The city famous for its skyline held buildings I barely knew.

I turned toward the glittering downtown to make sure I didn't miss the turnoff to Michigan Avenue. We passed what used to be Goodman Theater, now a dimly lit entrance behind what must be a new wing of the Art Institute.

Wide trenches where engines crawled on railroad tracks once defined Chicago's days as a hub of cattle and commerce. Though I didn't say it as I grew up, those tracks parallel to Michigan Avenue with their occasional inching engines were an expensive real estate tribute to the city's history. All that was gone now. In its place, a polished steel structure flowered at the center of a park, real estate now a gathering place and a monument to a different legacy of this region: architecture mixed with gleaming public art. It was as if what I didn't recognize brought me to memories and treasures I had stored and neglected, starting with a tiny childhood with my mother in a grey, stone apartment building on the Near North Side.

I remembered the strange order in the street names all around me in those days. We went to church and shopped at Saks on Michigan Avenue. A typical walk with my mother took us west on Division, left on State, forking left again on Rush for a hamburger at the corner of Bellevue or pancakes at the corner of Oak. From there we'd walk east, returning home on Lake Shore Drive, turning west onto Division, satisfied with our full circle. This patterned circle with a small park on Astor Street nearby was my world as a child.

Just outside this circle, the House on Un-American Activities hearings wound to a close in the former U.S. Court of Appeals building around the corner on Lake Shore Drive. Sometime later, I leaned into the almost-warm sand at Oak Street Beach, finding fleeting comfort as I pondered the assassinations of Martin Luther King and Bobby Kennedy. And after that, Grant Park erupted, barely containing protestors who challenged the morality of a war and were met with billy clubs and tear gas. It was in these places that history and personal story etched themselves forever into memory.

A new Michigan Avenue now shimmered before us as Julia and I drove north to our hotel. Despite the familiar presentation, I found that everything had changed, as if the years had picked up the stores I remembered and shuffled them like little blocks into new places on a board. Saks stood across the street from where it had been. The only familiar things in this place were street names I knew well and the anonymous sprawl of the brand-name stores found in every city.

Our hotel at the corner of Michigan and Delaware was exactly one block between Walton, where my mother lived when I was in college, and Chestnut, where she lived until I moved her to California. Fourth Presbyterian Church across the street looked and felt the same. Without going in, I knew the hard, wooden pews, the ever-present chill of stone floors and walls, the Anglican elegance of the woodworking on the pulpit above the congregation, and the hopelessness of Calvin's original doctrine of predestination. I could revisit those memories anytime without setting foot in the building. I gazed at my old church from the forgiven perspective of a different religion, one in which I was loved by God.

The next morning, Julia and I set out for Evanston, turning from Walton to Michigan Avenue and the Outer Drive. We passed a patchwork of snow and fencing where there is beach in the summertime, then a salt-stained, concrete walkway and later still a desolate harbor that I pictured full of boats berthed in their docks amid others anchored to brightly colored, bobbing moorings. The familiar high-rises on Lake Shore Drive ended where Lincoln Park began and then abruptly continued as we passed the harbor and continued north.

"You'll know we're in Evanston when we pass a lakefront cemetery," I told Julia.

Before long, we passed the cemetery. I thought to myself as I had hundreds of times before that, no longer would anyone build a cemetery on lakefront property.

"Your grandma wanted to buy a house in Evanston for years. She wanted to rent out rooms to students so she could "swing it"—her words for "afford the mortgage," I said a few minutes later. That's pretty much how the drive was, a running narration of what I remembered and what had changed. The houses along Sheridan Road in Evanston looked exactly as I had left them thirty years ago, yet I found myself thinking that most had without a doubt been renovated inside. Wide expanses of snowy lawn front and back were uninterrupted by fencing that is common in other parts of the country.

Julia and I liked to get to campuses well in advance of the tour to poke around for ourselves. We continued on Sheridan Road, reaching the campus and driving through it to Wilmette. Going around one corner, I said, "See that yellow house? Grandma tried to buy it twice. She really wanted to, but she couldn't swing it."

Sheridan turned again, and I said, "We'll go back in a minute, but I want to show you one thing."

Before us rose a white, filigreed dome with nine arches curving inward to converge at the top. The dome rested like the top layer on a larger structure and a still larger one that completed the wedding-cake architecture.

"It looks like the Mormon Tabernacle," said Julia.

"It's a different religion—Bahai'i."

"It's amazing. Now can we go into town?" she said, turning to the glowing screen of her cell phone, where a new speech bubble and a "ding-ding" had called her back to another conversation.

We drove to downtown Evanston on Ridge Avenue and jogged onto newly added streets framed by high-rises where there had once been low houses and stores.

"This is so cool, Mom."

I pointed out the signature Marshall Field's clock at the corner of Sherman Avenue, realizing that the building had been converted to a retail galleria with loft condos above the second floor.

"We should probably get to the visitor center." I spoke, realizing that the address said Hinman Avenue, not the administration building I had pictured on Clark Street. I raced through a mental map that seemed to fail me, trying to remember the location of a street I once knew well. North-south my mind told me as we drove east, and then we were there.

The tour was typical and not so: buildings, a summary of student life, a snapshot to be mulled and compared with other campus tours. The familiar grid now included buildings where there had been lakefront, land where there had been rocky waterfront. Once large buildings were dwarfed by newer, larger structures.

As we walked, I recognized the familiar and timeless: crisp air, whipping breezes, the white of dried salt on the sidewalks, the dusting of snow on lawns, a thick lace of leafless branches. It dawned on me that what happened inside the buildings was the same, a continuum of learning in every landscape.

Our tour guide steadily narrated buildings and classrooms, programs and majors, the library and student union, a philosophy favoring the liberal arts. Suddenly I realized that Julia was asking more questions than she had on any other college tour.

"Would you say this campus has a balance of academics and fun?

"Can you major in something else and still be on a pre-med track?

"Do you get used to the weather after a while?"

"Do you like the quarter system?"

We hadn't yet reached the visitor center when she turned to me and said, "I love it."

I looked at my blonde, green-eyed, California daughter who had inherited and improved on qualities of diligence, competitiveness, ambition, and high academic standards. I could see her thriving on this campus despite the weather. It could be a new generation of memories for me—a daughter in the school where her parents met years ago, the university her grandmother attended as well.

I wanted to do one more thing in Evanston before we left. We turned the car in the direction of downtown and drove south on Sherman Avenue, turning right on Lake.

"See that old house on the corner?" I pointed as I slowed the car. "That's where I had my first apartment in college."

"Unfortunate-looking building." Julia liked pretty houses, and this one was dirty frame and stucco.

Sadness and urgency rose in me as I repeated one word in my mind: "Reba."

I wanted to find Reba before we left town, to see the place where the best parts of my adult life began. We continued and soon reached Howard, putting us back in Chicago. I needed to find Reba Street before leaving Evanston. I turned west and then north on Ridge, passing a familiar hospital and street names. Reba was one-way in the direction I couldn't turn. I drove to the next block and turned right. A glimpse into an alley reminded me of snowy mornings when we would shake loose and lift the door of the rented garage so we could get in to warm up the Fiat. I drove to the corner and turned again, stopping at Reba.

It was a narrow street with cars on both sides, parked proof of many apartments. I looked at the red-brick building on the far right-hand corner and puzzled over fresh, black paint and shiny glass—new windows on a building I knew. I recognized that second-story bedroom window, the place of morning laughter and silly love, the kind that began a life together.

I looked to my left and easily found the three-story, wood frame house, the next apartment where love turned serious, we turned vegetarian, and, wondered what came after graduation.

"Dad lived there, and then he moved there," I gestured, pointing out the two buildings. "This is where we began."

Full, silent tears filled my eyes, tears for what was lost and what was yet to be lost, tears about change. I couldn't bring myself to turn onto Reba. I continued straight, passing the street I had searched for, heading back to the city.

"Could we shop a little, Mom?"

We left the car at the hotel garage and took off down Michigan Avenue, peering into windows, stopping to notice where familiar stores were newly placed.

"Where do you want to go?" I asked.

"Well, the only thing we don't have where we live is Saks, so let's go to Saks."

It was newly situated, vertical and narrow on a corner across from where it once dominated an entire block. We swung round the revolving door to be met by a blast of warmth and an offer of a perfume sample. Escalating up, we circled floors, pausing in denim—7 For All Mankind, Citizens of Humanity, Joe's Jeans, Rock & Republic, and True Religion.

"You don't have to follow me around, Mom."

As Julia stopped to hold an Alice + Olivia top to her frame before a mirror, I turned in the direction of Dior, where I ran my hand over the familiar patterns on my way to a deep, leather chair. In unspoken thoughts, I mused that the push to adulthood was equally matched by the way Julia relaxed into the comfort of her young age.

"Okay, I'm done. This Saks isn't even as good as the one in San Francisco."

"It used to be a wonderful store. Many of my clothes as a child came from Saks." I could almost smell the combination of radiator heat, genteel perfumes, and mothballs that produced treasures like shiny penny loafers, poofy crinolines, and a millinery department with seasonal displays of felt, straw and feathers. I looked at the surround of brand names, the stores of every city, and then at Julia.

"You look tired. Want to get a coffee?"

Julia perked up, grateful. We revolved into the cold and then into another blast of warmth and escalated to a wood-paneled restaurant in Nordstrom, where she ordered hot chocolate.

"What do you want to do tonight?" It was Valentine's Day, and despite my best efforts, we couldn't get tickets to Second City. We'd already seen Xanadu in New York before it toured to the stage a block from our hotel. Julia coughed hard and said, "I'm not feeling that good, Mom. Couldn't we please go home earlier tomorrow?

I had planned that we would stay in Chicago through the next day, leaving that evening. I felt a little surge of resistance to altering my plan. "I'll think about it. But what about tonight. What's your pleasure?"

"Let's just get food from the food court and watch a movie in our hotel room."

The food court a block from our hotel offered sushi, stuffed potatoes, stir-fry, soups, salads, and a deli case stocked with freshly prepared continental dishes. We made our selections, carried them to our room, and turned on James Bond.

The next morning, I awakened and went to get tea in the hotel lobby. We were clearly done in Chicago. A sense of urgency to get home had replaced my initial resistance to changing the plan.

Returning to our room, I picked up the phone. My laptop screen displayed six flights, one of which was nonstop and closer to noon, clearly the preferred choice to our 5 p.m. departure with one layover. After waiting through tinny music and occasional advertising for the airline, I spoke. "I'm interested in standing by for an earlier flight than the one I'm on and wanted to check seat availability."

"There are eight seats on the flight you want, and you will have to pay the difference between what you paid and the full fare that would be charged to you today."

I calculated the $250 upcharge for flying four hours earlier, and said, "No, I don't think I'll do that."

Julia, who had not stirred, now sounded groggy and nasal. "What about your frequent flier miles, Mom?"

I called back and was quickly connected to a crisp voice. "You don't have enough frequent flier miles, but you could pay fifty dollars to reinstate the free ticket that expired."

"So, I'd pay fifty dollars for one, cancel the existing ticket and pay a $175 total, which is a seventy-five dollar delta from the $250 I heard from the last agent."

"Delta? What does Delta have to do with it?"

"Oh, I wasn't talking about the airline. Delta as in difference—price difference—a savings of seventy-five from the $250 originally quoted."

"Well, no, actually. You'd cancel both existing returns and each of you would use one leg of your round trip to fly on the earlier flight."

So for fifty dollars, we would fly in three hours and arrive home six hours earlier. We scrambled to pack, shuffle the luggage with us to the checkout line, and collect the car. We would depart from Midway Airport, whose restoration in the last decades had made viable what I thought of as a rundown relic on the South Side, a shabby part of town.

We lifted our weekenders into the trunk and tucked ourselves into the cold car. I turned east and put us on East Lake Shore Drive for one more tour through the Loop, empty on this cold, Sunday morning.

"These train stations look pretty rundown, Mom. There's so much they could do to clean them up." Julia liked technology and polish. I well remember the dented metal stairs leading upward to dilapidated benches where passengers waited for the next "El." The wear of the stations seemed to match overcast weather and weary crowds. Newer stations were an unusual break.

We turned west on Randolph and circled the Civic Center Plaza and the Picasso statue that had long ago turned to a dull shade of rust from the orange color at its installation. Heading west on Randolph, I said, "This area used to be known as Skid Row. You had to lock your doors and be very careful because drunks would lurch into the street in front of your car."

I could see all that had been cleaned up. The once-faded brick buildings had been sandblasted to a true red with new windows and doors, lofts, and shops at the ready in yet another gentrified neighborhood.

Soon we were on I55, a highway I didn't know. I had no experience on those West Side streets, though my imagination easily conjured the old and rebuilt neighborhoods I knew were there—Polish, Irish, Italian, African American, Latino enclaves, a melting pot amalgam under flat, grey skies. Canal Street, Halsted, Archer, Ashland, Damen, Western, Kedzie, Pulaski to Cicero Avenue. I knew the names, the grid on which they were arranged, the strict shape of memory underlying all that had changed.

Dick, Reconsidered After Forty Years

The skies were clear when I landed, comfortable in the city I knew as a second home.

"I could meet you for a drink around nine tonight or for coffee mid-morning," I said from my seat behind the white-turbaned cab driver, who ferried me from JFK to midtown. Houses with wrought-iron fences and grey metal awnings blurred into high-rise brick projects with balconies and bars on lower-floor windows. Once through this worn landscape we would arrive in the shining city that long ago claimed me in the combination of my own memories and possibilities I imagined it held. I like the feeling that New York is a kind of home, holding past and future, memory and hope.

I settled into the plastic captain's seat of the van-cab, dialed the first number and began orchestrating my life as if it was important to slot people into hours and days. The voice on the other end of the phone opted for nine tonight and said he'd meet me in my hotel lobby.

It didn't take long to check in at the marble-and-mahogany reception desk, wheel my bag into the mirrored elevator and then my shoebox room, and change out of airplane-misshapen clothes. The phone rang. "Great. I'll be right down."

I rounded the dark, wood corridor to the lobby with its comfortable seating circle, groupings of Queen Anne chairs and overstuffed sofas around coffee tables.

Directly across the room, he was instantly recognizable. Enormous eyes. Gaunt face. He held a grey-flannel trilby in one hand, wore a saggy sport coat and a colorless Henley. His neck supported a narrow head with a receding hairline. The slim face surprised with small chipmunk checks at the jawline. Lips closed over teeth meant for broad smiles: his mouth seemed serious and sealed. I recognized everything I saw. He saw me and cracked a smile that got wider and wider—the smile.

"Dick, you look great."

We hugged after an awkward handshake.

"A hug was in the plan."

I was suddenly tired and took charge. "How about we have a drink here rather than trying to find someplace to go?"

We walked up small steps to the hotel lounge.

"I'm going to move my chair closer." Dick started moving a chair to the head of the table.

"Just sit here," I motioned to the chair next to me. We sat side by side, turned in our chairs to look at one another. The conversation started easily.

"I always see Greta when I'm in town, but this is a treat thanks to Facebook. Do you see Ron, other classmates?

"No, we talk from time to time. I haven't had the desire to track the others down."

"What about his sister? Do you follow Polly?"

"Totally. She's pushing the limits of theater. Everything she does is challenging and intelligent."

"I was sorry to miss her when she appeared at the San Jose Rep."

"She's on a different level."

"Do you go to high school reunions?"

"No, there aren't a lot of people I'd want to see."

I feel exactly the same way.

It's easy to keep talking and remembering. Innocent ambles along Lake Shore Drive, anonymous coffee shops, teenaged "schedules" to meet at someone's "co-op" (in the days before condominiums). It would most likely be at Greta's house, where there was the enticement of her father—a former World War II spy—and a smart, older sister, a role model for anyone aiming for Harvard.

He was still Dick, the incredibly good guy, whose smile squished from mouth to eyes to the ridge of the nose to the chipmunk cheeks back to the eyes. Forty years later, there was the smile with bright eyes that resolutely looked at me. "It's been forty years, and there aren't a lot of people I'd want to see."

*   *   *

I would lunch with Greta uptown the next day. She and I get together every time I'm in New York. She is a quiet cornerstone in my memories, the growing up ones from another time when change was a staple of my life. In those anxious high school days, I pushed old friends away reaching for new ones, only to re-sort the lineup and rotate in still different ones. I saw my teenage daughters do the same thing, and now understand that they create change somehow knowing the next wave will not be of their making.

The pull to touch the past is irresistible while considering the future. I find myself newly chatting online with old schoolmates, and meeting some again in person.

"Everyone who comes here is either gay or plumped up with collagen," she would say. "I like sitting up front. I thought you'd enjoy the scene."

I was in New York this time on business, a conference of professional peers from all over the world.

Later in the day, I sat in a room representing my once high-profile Silicon Valley PR agency—Silicon Valley, the capital of change. A fee-structure discussion pointed out to me that my company, once one of the largest, is now among the smallest in the group. The group itself has grown to include agencies from Europe, Eastern Europe, South America, Canada and Asia. There are the longstanding familiar accents: Canadian, Irish, English and "Y'all." We greet one another with effusive handshakes, hugs, and kisses on two cheeks that signify the world and ethic we share: compete, win business, shine with creativity and solutions, never bask in the glow of success, push on, accept setbacks, push on, and then when we come together, share everything we know. The public relations business can be tough and friends are good to have.

It's been two years since I attended one of these semiannual meetings, two years of economic crash, heart surgery, losing my husband to cancer. Two years of sea change. It is hard now to walk into a room full of people who want to talk about search engine optimization and social media. At times, I feel like an alien.

I'm past the stage of crying without provocation. I can say, "I lost my husband almost three years ago" to a total stranger without tearing up, and I can go on with the sentence.

I can hold up my end of the professional conversation, talking about best practices with clients, debate the demise of print media, invoke the merits of integrating social media into client communication campaigns, and advocate the benefits we offer our employees. Yet there's much newly in me that the listener cannot see, the door opened by death.

I am a single woman for the first time since I was twenty-two. My youngest daughter will go to college next year. I continue to run my husband's semiconductor company in addition to my own PR firm, and I have a quiet conviction about the question that I would not have been able to answer before cancer silently reset our lives. I knew I loved my family, but I did not then know what would feed me, sustain me beyond that love. Now, I vibrate with my own writing life.

In writing I have found the consuming joy of ever looking for what I cannot see, like the dust on the crown molding in my hotel room and traces of life particled in the carpet under my feet. I can't see the sewer under the street, only the steam that proves the swampy mess is there. I can't see the wind that I know is blowing, only the leaves that drop and bounce sideways over cars. I can't see drivers pushing brakes to the floor but know they have when the car stops. And I can't see the circumference of the Earth's rotation around the sun or the arc of the moon's rotation around Earth. I can't see God, only miracles. I can't see good, only goodness in people. I can't see the moment life begins in a human, an animal, a plant. I can't see power, only the result of it: the filling, rolling, falling of an ocean wave, the rising, conquering destruction of a dictator.

I can't see the thing that makes humans seek and stick to one another or the thing that strikes between people, breaking to shreds our own humanity. Nor the hating, the reconciliation, the healing, the hopeful return to wholeness. Yet I know that what I can't see is real.

Our conference group gathers in a genteel, sconce-lit, hotel meeting room, where an agency from Frankfurt applies for membership. Three fresh-faced thirty-somethings stand and wave curtly when their names are introduced. Each wears a dark suit, crisp, starched shirt and tie. As Helmut walks deliberately to the podium, I wonder if they will wear khakis and jeans like the rest of us once they are accepted into the network.

"Our three principals are…."

"Our turnover is…"

"And when my father retired he took over our financial operations." The PowerPoint covers all the facts with occasional illustrations of men in suits, a bull, and generic growth charts representing the firm's particular expertise in investor relations.

Next, we are introduced to Jim from Toronto, whose agency is also applying for membership.

"I come from a technology background and would like to attract some tech clients."

"As a representation of our work, I am showing shipping, education, and financial-services client work." Jim flips through his presentation showing a smart mix of print, television coverage and social media.

The applicants leave the room, we vote and rise to our feet, applauding our new members when they return.

I'm on the hunt, pitching and winning a new client over two meetings in a Queen Anne-seating quadrant of the lobby. I moderate a social media presentation and schmooze from table to table at the Cotton Club in Harlem, where our group adjourns for dinner.

"David, do you love this? It's like San Francisco!"

"John, this must be your daughter—she looks just like you—but pretty."

"Sandy, it's been forever. We have to talk."

"Uwe, Germany…Adam, so good to finally work with you."

I revel in competitive zeal, my own and that of my colleagues. We have gathered to discuss the future of our business together. I am not only considering the future they discuss, but my own.

I dislike having dropped from one of the largest to one of the smallest agencies in the group. My competitive nature whispers to me, insistent that I'd be crazy not to throw myself and my firm full force into the energy of this brotherhood.

Yet that quiet voice I have come to trust rises again, reminding me of the certainty of change, the strange gift from death that demands and proclaims new life. I am torn. Will the call to compete step in front of the hours I set aside for my quiet pursuit of what cannot be so easily seen, the thing I find in writing? Will the "old familiar" trump my newfound courage to meet change?

In this city that I call my second home, the city of my father, I return to cornerstones concealed long ago as I built my life with intention.

Greta will forever be the girl of Norwegian heritage, a heritage I share but keep in the shadows. She is a time-stamped sister with dark-water eyes, a quick smile, a rush of words, a stand-back watcher. She is high school, friendship going well, girl things gone awry, boys that get moved on a girly checkerboard, driving with the top down, blue eye- shadow and tight boots, mini-skirts and sailor pants. She is the one who after all those years remembered, stayed in touch, realized as I did that our selective human connection endured and is our structure and our certainty.

*   *   *

I fly out in a soupy fog.

Shifty weather had blown and slopped on and off for the last two days, sending sudden showers of brown leaves skidding along parked cars then skittering to concrete sidewalks and glistening asphalt from which passing cabs spray puddles into the air onto anyone within reach.

I had asked Dick the obvious question. "So any wives, any kids?"

"No," he answered A serious look at me and then a shy smile. "Relationships for sure, but, no, it got close sometimes but didn't work out. I guess that's a subject for therapy. I did have therapy."

"Was that a good thing?"

"Well, yes, but at a certain time I did it for a girlfriend. One day I went into the therapist's office and said, 'You know I'm stopping now.' "

"Why?"

"I felt like I'd done what I went there to do. The girlfriend thought it would make me a better boyfriend. I wasn't sure I needed therapy, but for a time it made me a better boyfriend in her eyes."

Dick's face squeezed into an incredible smile, his large features suddenly melted, confused, a generous spilling. He lifted his shoulders in a shrug and turned a relaxed unforeseen beam at me. I then remembered that he loved to make people happy and always smiled back at his friends in the days when we were kids.

Dick opened his wallet as we finished our drinks, and I saw a small, gold badge. He was sitting in the chair next to me. It was easy to reach over and touch the gold surface.

"Are you a deputy?"

"I volunteer as a defense counsel assistant. You remember my parents wanted me to be an attorney. It turns out I'm good at it." Dick was at the head of his class throughout high school.

"We all knew you would be," I said.

"I got to Harvard…and I realized I could never be that good at anything."

"College is a bigger world than high school, especially the one we grew up in." I took on a conciliatory tone at the same time, wondering why Dick's intelligence hadn't bolstered him against self-doubt.

"The people there far surpassed any capability I had," he insisted. Just maybe Dick had intellectual chops but not the cutthroat nature to give up his heart, and in some brave or incredibly instinctive adolescent act, he chose heart, the hard road, the street- corner reality of finding one's humanity another way.

"I didn't drop out or anything. That would've been wrong. I kept my covenant with my parents, but I focused on music and literature."

"Well the music business is tough—especially here in New York."

"The good thing about it is that there are so many specialties—little slices where one can really achieve something—a slice where you can get to the top."

So, that still mattered.

"You've certainly gotten some good press." In the weeks leading up to our meeting, NPR had run several stories on his release with Louden Wainwright, honoring the American folksinger Charlie Poole.

"I hired the right publicist. Those things don't happen without the PR people."

"Good move. You're right about that."

I stepped back into my professional mind to consider for a moment what it would be like to have Dick as a client. Would he come in with organized information? Would he use his considerable skill to have generated the written materials—releases, backgrounders, even pitches to media? Would he have strong opinions about which media venues were critical? Would he take counsel, try to rush the agency? I was pretty sure he'd interview well, and I was very sure he wouldn't say, "We have to get on Oprah."

As my plane made its way through the clouds, I was torn again. Everything had clicked right along: visits with friends, new client pitch, agency sessions, even my strategic exit to JFK with an Irish colleague. I was filled with the energy of our professional network, the power of being affiliated with fifty incredible, independent agencies in the image of my own. Formerly.

And then my mind's eye looked into Dick's pale, brown eyes where I found his spilling, squeezing smile, the goodbye hug. He smelled like hair, clothing with a lack of starch, and I think his embrace was a little noncommittal, as if hugging was not quite his thing. He had made life choices early on, hard ones, choices that I was only now contemplating. He stepped away from the track. Greta did not.

I will always visit Greta in honor of our girl days, our ability to talk about anything, and our mysterious bond.

A day later I posted a Facebook thank you to Dick.

"All that time and some things don't change—I enjoyed talking as much as in yesteryear. Thanks for fitting me into your evening.

Dick replied, "Me, too, but you know, I can't remember the substance of any of our conversations forty years ago. It's as if who we were in my memory was a locus of images and feelings of connection and attachment made no less real by the absence of specifics."

The locus of images and attachment—then and now.

The Paradox Formation

When I was a child, Moab terrain served as backdrop for macho trucks suddenly dwarfed like hood ornaments atop massive mesas, the sun blazing rays from which, within seconds, a Chevrolet logo would emerge.

In a photo of Moab terrain, Doug half-crouched with his bike on a flat rock precipice, the Colorado River murky in the canyon's distance below its edge. In the frozen moment, a smile spilled across his face completing the image of energy about to explode into motion. I chose this photo for the cover of his funeral program.

A year later, I drove past the entrance to Arches National Park, feeling its call, a mystical promise that some resolution could be found in this place. As winter stretched before us, the entrance soon behind us, I promised out loud, "I'll be back."

I landed in Las Vegas, finding my car.

Urban density and electric bling disappeared. I started into new terrain of sage dotting dusty flats from which rock rose, horizontally lined in layers etched by water and time.

I have always loved the smallness of cattle against mountains. My camera in hand, I alternately zoomed and widened its lens, taking shots as we passed through subtly changing landscapes. For one stretch, a succession of semis in primary colors lumbered uphill. My hand worked the lens to store those images. Continuing, I snapped a vein of blue mountainside, a snowy crater, dreamy shapes through a veil of field dust and striations of cloud patching over the sun.

It was only later, looking at many of these images that I said to myself, the landscape would not have its power without roiling clouds, clouds clinging to mountaintops, clouds breaking electric glare into bands of sweeping color, or a single wisp like a jet trail cocked at an odd angle, as if marking a particular point in the landscape.

Sorting through my own thoughts, I felt the landscape tease me ever closer to my destination with new offerings of color and rock formations. Green fields gave way to articulated layers of orange between which, houses and utility poles angled like glue-downs or afterthoughts. A sudden junkyard created a crop of metallic color behind barbed-wire fencing. Upward sweeps of charcoal—magnesium and other ores broke sandstone formations. A sudden stovepipe reached skyward above smaller, angled hills. Green showed above the charcoal, yet another mineral appearing in a red, mountainous stand. The sheer beauty of the place at once called me into the landscape and made a knot in my throat as I thought how much Doug loved this place, had returned to it, and would have liked to return with me.

A flurry of calls over my Bluetooth speaker interrupted my reverie. The sky blackened above. In the distance, rain clouds opened in all directions. I arrived and pulled in to sit out the storm at the condo to meet up with other friends who stayed there before we set up our own campground on the wet, red earth.

* * *

The wind and rain built in ferocity until the storm had emptied and exhausted itself. When the skies lightened again, we set out for the campground, laying tarps, erecting tents, and clustering supplies on the central picnic table.

The tent I had brought was a relatively new one Doug bought for its lightness, a requisite for backpacking trips. Having never used it, I had set it up at home to be sure I would know how it fit together should I have to set up in the dark. The stakes and collapsed poles I pulled from stuff sacks felt familiar. As I worked, I traveled the distance from growing up a city child to camping with Doug for the first time in college. How much had changed from those days of relying on his direction to choose the spot, clear debris that could pierce a tarp, and place the tent with poles and stakes that made a sturdy shelter! What I had learned from his love of nature was my own love of being there with him, my own love of being there.

I tossed the fly over the ridge, snapping it to the tent frame, stretching and securing its corners with stakes. I could almost hear him narrating proper setup.

Our activity took on a businesslike efficiency in the falling light. Nevertheless, I heard my friend, Simon, say, "This is the campsite we were in the last time we were here with Doug."

Simon pitched a central canopy and hung his solar shower from one pole, a ritual I imagined he and Doug also did years earlier. I carried on my preparations with a heightened sense of destiny, remembering the promise to come here, the knowledge that I would, efforts that at first failed, then the invitation to this trip and our arrival to discover that we camped in the exact place where Doug had been. For the rest of the week this would be home: it was a beautiful site.

The twenty x thirty patch of red sand was cornered on two sides by gently sloping, slick rock, making an easy climb to the higher, rounded ledges and the valley view. The sides not bordered by rock opened to the red sand expanse of the campground and mountain ridges beyond. Low, craggy trees and shrubs occasionally interrupted a landscape of red sand, dusty sage and desert wildflowers.

In the languid days that followed, I would shuttle bikers to departure points that had names like Porcupine Rim Trail. I'd decipher petroglyphs in plain view on roadside canyon walls, study improbable formations of towering sandstone from all angles, search endlessly for the next shot in my photo journal of this place.

It was easy to be caught up in palettes of siena, russet, auburn and orange. Common weeds at first glance produced seemingly infinite variations of the color green, from dusty blue-green to shimmery yellow-green. The landscape that holds dinosaur tracks is also home to *podistera eastwoodiae, oreovis bakeri, besseya alpina, saxifraga bronchialis,* and *carex perglobosa*—ten, imperiled plant species found only in this region. Each look through my lens, every shot I took, framed the story of another world.

Coexisting with what met the eye was that which remained below the surface concealed until the moment it exerted a different kind of power: quicksand and currents of the Colorado River, the highly venomous, protected midget rattlesnake; scorpions curled in the shelter of waiting shoes, compass cactus pointing southward, temperature swings of 70° in a single day, offering equal opportunity for dehydration and hypothermia. The beauty that met the eye was more than matched by the enormity of what one couldn't see in this land where certain soils weren't dirt but living soil crusts, land still forming.

*   *   *

In the 11 x 14 photo on my office credenza, Doug leaned against red rock that rose in an imperfect arch around him. Taken a few short years before his death, it is a shadowy shot unlike the many blazing vistas tourists have taken at this place. His fitness and strength seemed to blend into the terrain, a formation himself against the rock, smiling his happiness there.

Now I walked uphill with determination, feeling my tennis shoes and wishing for the steadiness of hiking boots. This was nothing, a climb everyone and their kid was doing. I ran for a bit to see how I felt. Nada. I was frisky as a kid.

Suddenly the casual atmosphere changed. People above me peered through an arch. They spoke French. I understood, but they didn't know it. He had a fear of heights but had scaled the slope to aim his lens through a layered rock arch. He was nervous as a pacing French *chat*, "Got the shot, got the shot, can't come down. Will you run my lens up here? No, I want to come down."

She didn't like heights either, held the lens, standing very still and did not look up at him. Not at all.

I paused there. The rock was flat and dusty. Many people—families with small children—passed me on their way down the mountain. I went up, saw the precipice, turned around and walked down.

I wondered if avoiding the embarrassment of telling the story could propel me on the path along the precipice.

I would have to tell Simon's wife, Sally, who hung below with six-year-old Abby. I was certain they could not make it to where I was. A six-year-old for a few miles on hot rock, after all.

I went uphill again to the place where the narrow path rounded the mountain on the right, canting inward to the wall. The edge and vertical drop made me stop. I tried touching the rock wall to my right, small comfort that held me against the dizzying impulse to tilt in the direction of the cliff. All I saw was cliff. I turned around, hiking all the way to the flat-rock meeting ground where up-comers met the down-goers. I planned my story to Sally. Suddenly, there she was.

Six-year-old Abby said, "I have a plan."

We walked the rocks, passing many down-goers, soon reaching my point of not going on.

"Put on your hat, Mary. Turn the left brim down."

"Watch my feet, Mary. That's the plan: watch my feet." Abby placed herself in front of me, and I walked fifty terrifying paces along the path's steep cliff, my eyes riveted to a pair of small, pink Crocs.

We reached the rock clearing, heard multilingual chatter in hushed voices punctuated by giggles and shrieks of children darting around the crowd. Delicate Arch rose before us, orange in the afternoon glow.

*   *   *

Just weeks before leaving on this trip, I had a dream that started in the family room of our home. Doug and I cocooned there, surrounded by redwood, a river-rock-mountain-cabin feeling without a fire lit in the fireplace. We spread ourselves on the big soft couch, draping limb over limb, dropping into the cushions, drifting into the sleep of utter contentment together.

Suddenly, I decided that I needed something from our bedroom, and I walked the length to the other end of our house. Opening the hall door, I heard a sound. It was a sound I heard earlier in the day in the same part of the house. I searched the two bedrooms on either side of the hallway and inspected the closets. I gave up and turned to continue to our bedroom.

I heard the sound again and turned back, this time, noting a sheet draped over the glass shower door in the hallway bathroom.

"Who's there?"

The sheet moved in the way of someone trying to be still, not breathe.

I pulled the bathroom door shut and held it tight. I tried to scream, but I heard only a gurgle before my throat closed. I tried again this time calling, "Doug."

The prolonged syllable of my hoarse yell took me from sleep to wakefulness, the sound building as I became more alert.

I had again come face to face with my own paradox: through all finality a lingering disbelief that death could take my husband who was so full of life—his absence from what I did juxtaposed with his presence in thought and memory. I realized that for all the ways in which I embrace life, I will never say goodbye.

It was after this dream that I came to a decision about the urn in my bedroom. Doug expressed his own rapture on various hikes and mountain treks by saying to whomever was nearby, "When I die, I want my ashes scattered here."

After his funeral, nephew Doug had asked for some ashes to scatter. I was not ready to part with them then. Moab would be the perfect place to start.

I drew the velvet sack over the pale marble urn, pulling its gold drawstrings tight and making a loose bow of them. A short drive took me and the urn I carried through the double doorway of the funeral home. To the left of where I stood, incense and ethnic music wafted from a memorial service in another language. After a short wait and my explanation that I would like some of the ashes distributed into the six small boxes I carried with me, I heard the words.

"I'm so sorry, but the urn is sealed. If we'd known we could have…."

The conversation replayed in my head for the rest of the day. The following morning I called back, the good consumer ready to talk. "I'd like to speak with a manager."

"The manager isn't in, but I am the senior person here. My name is Valerie. How may I help?"

"I came in yesterday, hoping to have some of my husband's ashes distributed from his urn into boxes. I was told it could not be done without shattering the urn because it's sealed."

"Yes, the cremains are handled according to…"

"I'm not implying that they were handled improperly. I didn't know that I had to say I wanted to have access to them later."

"They're first sealed in plastic…."

"How was I to know? I was not advised that there were different sealing techniques if one wanted access later—if one had plans to…"

I was no longer the good consumer. Valerie heard my gasp as I stopped talking. Her smooth-as-an-undertaker voice took over.

"I'm so sorry. I lost my husband seven years ago, and I truly understand. I can check with our manager and call you Monday."

"I won't be here. I was planning to take ashes on my trip."

"I'm so sorry. I will nevertheless talk with the manager and call you a week from today. Will that work?"

Her promise ended the conversation, leaving me saddened that I would not fulfill some shadowy promise made more to myself than to Doug.

*   *   *

"Trrrrrrooeeeee, Trrrrrroooeeeeee," split open the darkness, shattering stillness.

"Trrrrrrooeeeee, Trrrrrroooeeeeee," lacy arpeggio through misty air.

"Trrrrrrooeeeeee…"

"Hah-hah-cah."

"Trrrrrrooeeeeee."

"Hah-hah-cah." Bigger, definite.

"Rooo-upt." A voice from a middle branch.

"Hah-hah-cah." I pulled my sleeping bag to my ears.

"Trrrrrrooeeeeee."

"Roo-upt."

"Trrrrrrooeeeeee. Trrrrrrooeeeeee."

"Hah-hah-cah."

It was like jazz. One instrument picks up on the fading resonance of another. The collection of them blend. Music runs its own course. When I listen to jazz, I don't wish for earplugs. Instead, I drink in soul-stirring colors and rhythms—ensemble awakening my senses with daylight.

I cracked open one eye, finding a sky the color of dark steel. The musk of dew reached my nostrils through an open vent. I closed my eyes, knowing when I opened them again, the sky would be a lighter gray glare with pinks and oranges creeping in bands behind clouds.

"Trrrrrrooeeeeee. Trrrrrrooeeeeee"

"Wra-dooo." A retort.

"Roo-upt."

"Wra-dooo."

"Trrrrrrooeeeeee."

"Hah-hah-cah."

"Wra-dooo." The last word.

I wasn't willing to give up sleep and tried to hold onto the dream I was already forgetting. In its place now I saw huddled shapes, upright specters on craggy branches outside my tent.

"Morning, all; morning, all."

"I need a worm, need a worm, need a worm."

"Morning, all."

"Quiet!"

"Damp here."

"Morning, all; morning, all."

So far, each voice took its turn, a teasing conversation, a community. They seemed to have personalities. My imagination in full swing, I couldn't get back to that dream. Maybe if I had earplugs.

I opened one eye, finding the glare I expected.

"Hah-hah-cah. Hah-hah-cah."

"Wra-dooo."

"Hah-hah-cah.."

"Roo-upt."

"Yaah-haak!"

"Hah-hah-cah. Hah-hah-cah."

"Yaah-haak!"

"Wraah!" An outlier.

"Hah-hah-cah."

"Roo-upt." Still making nice.

"Wraah!"

"Yaah-haak!"

"Wra-dooo. Wra-dooo,"

"Yaah-haak!"

With each band of color and brightening cloud, the racket reached a more urgent cacophony of trills, nasal hacks, atonal spits, tenor urps, and belligerent retorts. With screeching crescendos, sound and light moved across the skies, breaking stillness, demanding that everything be changed—all at once. And then, something monumental happened.

On the horizon, the round, hazy light stretched its glow, repainting the sky, seeping warmth between cracks of night, releasing from dew a savory waft of cactus flowers, blue-tinged shrubs and red sand dust. Everything became silent.

Breaking sunlight breathed a beginning, day in place of the dream I lost.

*   *   *

It wasn't until I returned home and slid into the slick, leather chair in the family room that I began my work. The chair was smooth, familiar. Outside the windows, a workman's power washer sprayed debris off the flagstone porch. I breathed in the wet mist, and the green stuff—moss, a mix of leaves, the bay tree—I slid sit bones into sewn leather as I began a search to find out what 500 million years of geologic changes had made into the place called Moab.

Within minutes, I was reading about periods of time: the Pennsylvanian, Permian, Priassic, Jurassic, Cretaceous and the Tertiaries, one, two, and three, each spanning hundreds of million years. My mind began to construct a time-lapse animation in which ocean waters covering eastern Utah flowed out, and shale and rock formed and layered onto one another, only to be covered again by ocean.

At one point, deep dunes formed into Navajo sandstone.

In another era, fine-grained Estrada Sandstone added its orange glow to the layers with hard, white Curtis sandstone capping some formations.

The Wasatch fault lines that divide Utah slumped on the eastern face, allowing sea waters to flood in yet again, filling the region with sediment that became a riverbed covered over in the pastel shale that now memorializes dinosaur footprints.

Yet again, eastern Utah became shallow ocean surrounded by western highlands and the Colorado Plateau. Toward the end of the Cretaceous era, the western edge of the continent began a massive uplift, the underground salt dome raising land. In fact, if one were to look beneath the shifting surface of the earth, a thick but unstable deposit of salt moved at glacier speed, the agent of change.

As the continent continued to rise, the Colorado River cut its course toward the Pacific Ocean, joining on its way with the Green River.

In what I imagine as a great heaving motion, the glacier of unstable Paradox Formation salt squeezed into a dome raising the rocks above it, creating an anticline as the Colorado cut deeper between the rising rocks. Fissures in the rock over this salt dome formed fins and arches that, once etched by water, would continue to be etched by wind. At some point, the center of the anticline collapsed as the salt eroded, likely dissolved deep into rock with the help of water running through fault lines at either side of the Moab Valley.

With time and image compressed in my brain, I paused my search, clear in my mind now: the vast sweep of change.

Evermore and Goodbye Again

Two days of orientation with Julia on the oceanside campus that would be her new home. I tried to appear calm. Topics included classes and credits, how to deal with your child leaving home, exposure to drugs, alcohol and sex. The Santa Barbara culture, campus safety, transition in study habits, things not going as your student expected.

On the way, freeways took us through low towns with sprawling car dealerships and slightly taller hospitals, the prison town that houses RFK's assassin, generous expanses of golden grass, grazing cattle, and rolling hills where we lost our radio reception.

We emerged after some miles of turns and valleys to an ocean view, a ripple of blue that lazed to the horizon.

The freeway passed a vacation spot and then cut inland to long stretches of geometric vineyards. After a hairpin turn around a craggy hill, the ocean opened before us. Radio reception returned us to NPR. We drove until we saw the newly familiar signs for an airport, a university—the turnoff.

I could not have planned for this moment.

A high energy academic, Julia spoke in superlatives about school from an early age, "I have the best teacher. I read the entire thing and it was *sooo* good. I can't wait to learn times tables—and algebra!" While other children cried at the curb about going to school, she bolted from the car to get to class. She had wanted extra math, extra writing—*extra,* just because. She hadn't changed as a young adult and was the first to admit, "Let's face it, Mom. I'm weird. I love school, and I can't wait for what comes next."

She awakened for Saturdays of her dad coaching her soccer team and later took up mountain biking and hiking. She resisted the idea that anything could go wrong for her dad until it was clear that his bony frame held only a fading smile and love, and that his spirit would endure with his wishes for us. She was my youngest. She slept on her dad's side of the bed for months after he died, crawled in the night before her departure for college.

We left home on the lingering anniversary of his diagnosis, another marking of days and hours, sadness.

Somehow, she held onto her joy, shattered though she was. Immediately after her dad died, she disappeared into her closet bawling into her phone. She emerged straight-faced and brave enough to read at the memorial service before a gathered group of five hundred people. She seemed too strong, too unflinching. It seemed that she only touched her grief occasionally, most often, instead, consoling me.

Now I sat on a low wall built of square cinder blocks, remembering the days when cinder blocks were a component of furniture in my own student apartment and on low walls separating dorm pathways from flowerbeds on a different campus long ago. A breeze from the ocean flipped my hair over my sunglass lens. Though gentle, it carried a cold that reminded me of stiff gusts from Lake Michigan in my college days. Manicured palms stirred and wisped upward from golden stucco walls lining the wide path to Carrillo Dining Commons. I noticed the absence of ivy and brick.

The lazy calm of a campus lacked the dense pack of bicycles that was usual between classes, table stands of advocacy groups and resonant echoes of human voices in the outdoor mall between buildings.

Groupings of fresh-faced freshmen clustered from one hall to the next. Organized groups of parents followed a student leader, trying to look calm about the child leaving their familial home, to follow roads of their own choosing. I seemed among the nonchalant. I was not calm.

I walked the paths, smiling at her enough times I hoped, and admired to both of us Julia's admission as an honors student. I shifted in my shoulders. Parents were presented with the topics of rape, drugs and alcohol, cautioned that our student may have a full grade point less in college than in high school. The state budget crisis, increased tuition fees and mandated furloughs were raised as topics against whispered subtopics of undergraduate research, honor's tracks and four-year graduation. I had been dreading this change.

I couldn't be still in my skin, because I loved her dearly, had to send her forth from her personal tragedy to a new world. Doug and I had raised her for stability, sound thinking and discernment in all situations where she would have to make a choice. The dean of the college told us that at this age decisions are sometimes by the moment. That was my greatest hope and fear. Most of all, I hoped we, as parents, had given her the resilience to stand back, choose wisely–and consistently.

I felt compelled to leave. I had done my part on campus and could opt out of the scheduled social stuff with strangers.   I reached the freeway with surging sadness. I missed her already and would in the days ahead. All our days together had delivered us to this one.

Ocean tides would roll in and out on the campus shores as she traveled the roads into adulthood. I told myself she will do well. Life can still be still her plum.

I wakened feeling like a cloud still had me, or like I could sleep more. My bed still belonged to two people, the heaviness of loss, my own thinning memories of once feeling so loved, and wonderment about living as a single woman in a world of couples. Singleness is cold air, closing the car door, returning home to all that used to be there, and turning in. Tomorrow brings change. Again.

Overlooking the Pacific across town from her campus on my last morning, I had been awakened by shouting—words I could not yet make out. Rambunctious kids playing on the lawn under my hotel room? The shouting continued as I stretched and shifted the six pillows at my head and rolled under duvet fluff. Finally, succumbing to morning, I drew back two sets of curtains, turned the latch, lifted and opened the heavy patio door. Stepping onto a narrow balcony, I looked down at the lawn three stories beneath me finding no one.

"You talk shit about me. You talk shit about me and people laugh."

My eyes traveled from the lawn below across the road toward the beach. On the sidewalk opposite me, a woman in dark hoodie and bright red pants thrust her whole body into a man going face-to-face and wagging her finger. I could hear his deep voice, much quieter than hers, words I couldn't make out, next to them a shopping cart filled and covered with a black tarp.

"You talk shit about me. You do, you do."

I looked up and down the beachfront road. Dense fog everywhere made whispers of limby palm trees and completely hid the sandy beach beyond a verdant crest of ice plant lining the path parallel to the ocean.

Every so often the day before, Julia had scrutinized me and asked, "How are you feeling about all this now?"

Although I had chest pains in the prior days, it was easy to focus on her excitement and even be swept up in it. She had packed with a great deal of planning and list making, saying, "Mom, we've got a lot to do tomorrow."

That morning, I had dressed and walked into the fog, crossed the street ready to join the walkers, runners, bike riders, doggy people, geriatric athletes, and garbage pickers on the ocean path. Dense but not cold, moisture hit my lungs. Runners passed me with snippets of conversation from behind that trailed off ahead of me, "She keeps saying we have to get them together for a play date, and I think so but is she just going to drop the kid off and…."

Oceanside, across the ice plant strip that separated sidewalk from sand, I recognized the black hoodie with her companion, the two who had been my wake-up call. They squatted, seemingly oblivious to life around them, now quiet. To my right, under well-spaced palm trees, a grassy lawn made a soft surface for runners protecting their knees, and a promenade for pure breeds: Corgi, Afghan Hound and prancy, manicured Standard Poodles. On the other side of the lawn, another sidewalk ended at a curb. Two dilapidated RV campers with sooty windows, faded paint and oilcloth curtains parked between cars. A folding chair and makeshift carpet were set up outside the door of one of the campers.

Across the street, the Fess Parker Doubletree sprawled an oversized city block. So the homeless folks have the better view, I thought to myself.

I continued on, stopping momentarily to take pictures with my phone: palms in fog, people silhouetted ahead. Another group of beach campers, their stories told in street-worn clothes, stubble, tangled hair and craggy teeth. There were six or eight clustered together, quiet—a family or community of sorts. I reached Stearnes Pier across from State Street. Within minutes I had tea in hand and walked out onto the pier.

Just offshore, barely visible in the fog, I made out a small canoe with a single figure hunched in a silhouette. A fishing pole arced off one side of the boat. I could easily have missed this solitary fisherman, so dense was the fog.

Even unseen, he would have been there, at work catching fish that were most certainly below the opaque surface. I drew closer. It was a morning to consider the seen and the unseen: a community of casual opulence disregarding the homeless beach-squatters trolling their perimeters. It took only another moment to realize that I was at work, searching a different opacity.

*　　*　　*

I, too, went to college that year in a place where the water of a strait, fine beach sand and strewn wood could be seen from the road. Ferries and cargo ships chugged across blue-scape. Snow-blanketed mountains rose in the east and the west. Olympics. Cascades. Walking up the beach at low tide, I found the mountain to the north, snow-covered in summertime, Rainier undulating to 14,411 feet.

My flatland citadel indulged corners of the soul most trampled in a working life—the press of must-do's, friends and family, no matter how beloved. This was a place of people I would not encounter, not think to seek out in my everyday life. Here are sisters, brothers, sages, guides, mentors.

The old fort setting stretched serene with grassy expanses, turn-of-the-last-century wood frame officers' housing. Iron doors, now padlocked, once opened to passageways inside gun batteries. What living men ran through those passageways? What untold stories had melted into walls firmed by hillside rock and dirt?

There was no fighting, and no one had died in battle here. Trails wind through shade of ancient redwoods, home to nesting eagles and red fox, and more concealed battlements where troops could position for defense of coastal waterways. At one corner of the fort's woods lies a small graveyard with uniform white markers, symmetrical in grass greened by rain. This is a federal cemetery. Men who served here earned the privilege of burial. A glazed, black cannon at the center honors and defends. It is both compact and somber, a tribute to those below—an innocent given wars now fought with IED's and land mines, suicide bombings and terror attacks.

For just a week I called this my campus, a fortress of poetry, the study of written word, reading, endeavor of expression. The rest of the work completed from home.

Writers can't write without traveling cavities only accessed in moments of silence and contemplation. In this place, I felt called.

Doug had trekked the verticals of the Olympic Mountains in healthy days before his death. I felt his spirit steady me from pristine peaks, silhouetted slopes above the buildings of this fort, above the lace of ancient trees in evening sky. Copper streaks between cloud strands.

I felt called here as if always a part of this place, an old soul now among other old souls—perhaps from shared pasts. I was infected, wanting sweet contagion of place and people, word pouring forth.

At the end of my week, I left that place where mountains hide and appear from clouds on three sides of me, depending.

There I said goodbye.

Entering The Space

I am drawn to a makeshift altar in one corner of Michael's living room. Upon the dark, closed cabinet rest several crystals, a ceremonial Navajo hot pad, a photo of the woman I will never know walking away from the camera on a sunny forest path, and a square, glass container holding a bouquet of turkey feathers, rattles of unknown native American origin, a sage smudge stick, some smaller feathers and a jumble of shells, stones, and other talismans. That corner radiates energy, loss, and stories that rest in what is preserved that she left behind.

In the serenity of this room, ochre mahogany bends cold light into shades of comfort. The leather warmth of chairs and couch rest on bamboo purposed anew that butts against earth rock on kitchen floors. The colors and geometries of a large area rug complement the palette of the room and signal what was carefully chosen for their world —his and hers—their trysting place. Melinda has been gone for two years.

I enter, knowing that his loss was as life-altering as my loss of Doug six years ago, knowing that we have both been broken and have wondered how to live.

Somehow, after the years that passed for each of us, we looked past our daily business together, seeing possibility in one another, testing and finding something new—a happiness that could be ours.

Still, our abiding love for spouses claimed by cancer walks with us each day we live, the sadness ebbing and flowing on anniversaries, in songs and poetry, on the lips of friends, and in the wistful eyes of young adults who shouldered their loss as children. These spouses will always be in us, for truly, we both had marriages that were not meant to end.

I approach the altar cabinet with feelings of curiosity and respect, drawing close but not touching the crystals before me. I have been told that they remember her and hold space for a long time, that I might speak directly to them and ask questions or give respects–and that they might be waiting for someone to clear them in an honoring ceremony. Despite the energy I feel there, I am surprised that it is not stronger.

He comes up behind me. "Yes, these are her things."

He moves the crystals like checkers and explains that the rattles are meant to be used together not individually.

I turn to him. "Did she say anything about the crystals?"

"No, not really."

"I have been told that they hold space…stories…."

He answers immediately. "Oh, I had a friend of Melinda's—another shaman—come to the house. Four or five of the crystals went away. She said some needed to go to another healer, and I wasn't meant to have one of them. She went through them all.'

I hug him hard and I'm sure he's baffled. "I'm so happy you did that."

How can he know the respect and relief I feel that he would take such care with her sacred objects? In that simple act, he released those crystals, their past, and set his intention toward the present.

I invite him for a weekend at my mountain cabin. On the day we are to leave, I first attend a memorial service for Peter, a friend and competitor, who died in a freak accident. He was eulogized in metaphors of light and salt—brilliance and essence—a man who made the most of every minute. His memorial was an ending, the afterglow of a life.

We arrive at the cabin after a three-hour drive, pushing through suburban and orchard landscapes to the Sierras, where the climb on the tree-lined freeway takes us past umber rock to limestone peaks and glimpses of mountain lakes. The changing terrain and passage of hours signal our transition from high-impact lives to this place where our singular focus might be the slow inhale of clean air, hearing birdsong, or warming cold extremities by a crackling fire.

This cedar cabin has been a citadel where our family has gathered for many years, in many permutations. In the beginning, Doug and me with a newborn and a two-year- old. Through the years our girls traced snow angels, slid down icy banks, skied, swam the lake, paddled canoes to the tiny beach, tossed tennis balls to dogs ready to swim for the fetch. We hiked to Crow's Nest and Peter Grubb hut, snowshoed to Mary Lake, cross-country skied through Royal Gorge, schussed the slopes of Sugar Bowl. Doug mountain-biked the American River Canyon, Hole in the Ground, and other trails with less illustrious names. Family and friends trekked with us to the cabin for Thanksgivings that might be California temperate or Sierra winter. As the girls became immersed in young adult lives, the cabin collected family for reunions and friends who rode with Doug, skied with both of us, and basked with us under nighttime skies that are dense with pinprick light.

It was important to me, for reasons I had not yet articulated, to bring Michael to this place. I unlock the door, turn on lights at the panel, open shades, light the fire in the upstairs stove—perform the rituals of opening my cabin–opening. This is my ritual akin to the shaman sorting through the crystals and taking certain ones to new healers. In the opening, taking in and sending forth, we make new lives, see the person we have always been and the one we are becoming. The actions of opening the cabin, though familiar, also felt brand new.

We walk in the late-afternoon light, letting exuberant dogs lead us around the snowy lake where, in the dead of winter, people snowshoe and ski. Now hints of spring have melted the shoreline to water again, and usually high snowbanks are shrinking into the dirt below them. A new season opens before us, despite the evening chill.

In the days that follow, we meander the historic part of Truckee, drive the mountain pass to Donner Lake, examine the trailheads at Royal Gorge, set out seed for the wild birds, feed the fire and admire flames that dart up around the logs we poke. We talk in hushed tones about being alive.

"Why are we here if not to evolve?"

"There is a space between what happens to us and how we react. I try to linger in that space."

After a long silence sitting as close as we can get to one another, I sigh in some kind of acknowledgement of the past this cabin holds for me, the sadness that lifts but returns at unexpected times.

"I didn't know how it would feel to bring you here."

"I knew this was important to you, but I didn't get it until I got here."

I feel a new certainty as our talk turns to travel we have planned, the comfort of the fire, and antics of restless dogs.

We talk easily about any subject, but we avoid one word except in the context of dark chocolate, windy cliffs overlooking a frothy ocean, tender hugs after urgent lovemaking, Sonny Rollins' saxophone licks and Joplin's raspy rendition of "Summertime." Perhaps we are conflicted—as if our acts of love must be well separated from being in love. Or is "being in love" never again to be except with the spouse who is gone?

Yet, love firms between us like a fragile bridge connecting two cliffs— to be trusted as it moves in the breeze.

Our Ventana

The day begins with sunshine and soft breezes, proclamation of spring out of season in what should be a California winter. Neither of us has slept well, perhaps because of a bad Chianti, a salty meal, or some unsettled expectation of the weekend itself. After morning routines, we load backpacks into the car and take off with the convertible top down. En route, I call a daughter, change theater tickets, check travel details for an overnight trip next week. I have worried about this weekend because he wants to take me to the place where your ashes are buried. Though the conversation is mundane, I feel myself retreating into a sense of reverence for the unknown to come. Turning onto the road to the coast, our conversation slows as we pass artichoke fields and the occasional trailer park.

In photos, your face is round with auburn hair and many looks. Sometimes the hair is pulled straight back in simplicity that shows large, brown eyes, a smile that belies both reserve and willingness to enter the moment. Other times the hair cascades around your shoulders in large curls, a length and softness often stereotyped as ultra-feminine. Still other times, you have light bangs and somehow look more Latina, as if the shadows cast by your hair darken skin and eyes.

And there are your characters—Carmen Miranda in headdress that is abundant with tropical fruit, and the tapered dress scantly draping a curvaceous body. Diana in Chorus Line, Sally Bowles in Cabaret, Mazeppa in Gypsy. Once I wondered what your voice sounded like and listened to the recording of the "Counting Song" from Rap Master Ronnie. It is said that in your day, you were a triple threat—acting, singing, and dancing onstage all the while teaching your "kids," and later choreographing shows on cruise ships.

We pass through busy Monterey traffic, merge into the narrowing road through Carmel, and push on to our destination in Big Sur.

Just last night he told me you selected the place where your ashes would be buried—the place called Ventana, which means "window"—and you specified a small pond with the ocean beyond.

He has told me of his solo trip there last year, of the many bird feeders that people have brought to the clearing where, three years ago, he traveled with family and friends to conduct a memorial, bury your ashes and honor your wish to be in the place where your spirit would "pass through the window." He showed me the photo of your name as he traced it in the dirt with twigs and spoke in happy tones about the many hummingbirds that are drawn to the place.

After some brief chatter about the bank of fog stretching inland to the coastal mountains and the proximity of the Continental Shelf to Carmel Beach soon behind us on the right, I ask, "Was that her personality to organize and direct things as she did her own memorial?"

I have come to know your house—the chairs where you sat, the bed where you slept and made love, your desk and its display of miniature Buddhas you collected. I have looked through your books on shamanic practices, curative Chinese recipes, the history of Broadway, Toltec practice, and healing with the five elements. I have stood in silent reverie, looking at your crystals, feathers and rattles—inspirations and remedies of the shaman you became. Your house was tidy—a reflection of a life lived on the move, and later kept in readiness for people who came to you for healing and bodywork.

Television played throughout the day when you were home alone, yet you were an avid reader. You loved movies but hated violence and would walk out to read in the theater lobby. You loved a good hotel room and were not much of a camper. You lost a pregnancy and nearly your life. I'm told you did not identify yourself as a mother type anyway. You lived close to your sister and maintained strong relationships with hundreds of cousins, uncles, and aunts. You entertained on a wooden platform built low to the ground encircling a huge avocado tree that shaded most of your backyard. I know all of this from your husband.

"No," he answers considering the anomaly. "No, in fact the opposite. She was pretty far along in her shamanic work by the time she became ill, and she was very comfortable with what she knew of 'the other side.' I'm not sure how hard she fought or if she felt attached to this life."

He has said this before.

The two of you kissed on your first date at a Neville Brothers concert, and he was certain you would have a life together. By that time, both of you had come through marriages to spouses who had been unfaithful. You produced shows on cruise ships together, moved across country, and you transitioned from performing to choreography and then the healing arts. His job took you back to the west coast— nearer to your mother and nephew who battled cancer—one would survive; one succumbed.

Telling your husband that he did not get a vote since he was never home, you got a dog. You trained the dog impeccably. You lost your dancer's trimness and said you wanted to lose ten pounds. You were a devoted wife to a husband who often worked long hours and nights. You trusted him, and he was faithful and adoring. The pictures from that time show a thoroughly comfortable, married couple. You traveled less and were alone more. You were close to immediate family in the way that relatives come together and push apart. I do not know who your friends were. I wonder how lonely you were, and if you spoke of it.

You were peace-loving and non-confrontational—seemingly not at all jealous, possessive or insecure. You eschewed business and have been credited with making art in all you undertook. You didn't have a temper; you had chronic fatigue syndrome. You didn't make a practice of rigorous exercise; you walked. You made plans to move again and start a business together; you were diagnosed.

"She worked with her healer down here and her other healers on her plan for her ashes."

Patches of murk and shine mottle the grey ocean simmering under vaporous cloud. As the road pitches between north-facing and south-facing turns, we slow behind drivers who brake constantly, as if a steady speed would be dangerous. Minutes later a waning sun breaks through, white lighting eastern-facing trunks, branches, and detritus of towering eucalyptus trees.

I have stepped into a space that you vacated, becoming friend, lover, and mate to the man you left behind.

We are at a new moment, in our odd way joined—though you will never know me —never look into my green eyes, nor I into your brown ones in a conversation that reveals our differences and similarities. We have an unfortunate convergence: my birthday is one day before the anniversary of your death.

I have thought all these thoughts in the months, weeks and days before this weekend, one in which he and I will travel to Big Sur. We have billed it to friends who know the ironic coupling of these days as a "celebration of life"—both mine and yours.

We continue in silence, soon reaching the roadside inn where we will spend the night. After check-in and inspection of our modest, oak-paneled room, we are back in the car.

"Let's go to Nepenthe." He looks at me, already in motion. Only later will I understand Nepenthe as the drug described in Homer's *Odyssey* as banishing troubles or grief.

A short distance later, we pull into a dirt parking lot. "I'd like to get a little something to put there."

He is speaking almost to himself as he locks the car, and then as an afterthought looks at me, "Do you mind if we go to where she is?"

"Not at all." His urgency is palpable.

It is the reason we are here, I think to myself, acknowledging my own colliding feelings. On one hand, this is their time and their place—and on the other, he has brought us together, the three of us, for reasons yet to be known.

We circle the gift shop, finally finding a small tin and wicker rattle, which he pronounces perfect and buys. We walk the stairs to the restaurant and its view of the ocean and Big Sur to the south. Crows cluster in near oak branches and a turkey buzzard circles and circles, waiting for scraps below. Beyond the steep slope from the decks where we stand, I see a brambly barrier to Highway 1 that opens to a green meadow, a small pond and the ocean beyond.

"That's it." He speaks very quietly at my side. "That's where she is. Just up from the grassy area. She wanted a pond with the ocean."

I have already taken pictures of the turkey vulture in flight, the coastal vista, and the murder of crows. "Take a picture of that, will you? I'd like to send it to a few people."

I frame the spot tight in my viewfinder. Then I turn the camera and take a shot of the two of us. We smile uncertain smiles—my interpretation as I review the photo. I wonder what it will be like to walk in the Ventana meadow below us.

Back in the car, I ask, "What does the rattle mean to you?"

"It's the presence of the spirit. When I came last year I left a little rattle, too." A gift—and a call to her spirit.

"The rattles have less meaning for me," he continues. "They're shamanic symbols for the spirit."

Redwoods and eucalyptus stretch tall and canopy the road as we reach a turnout just around a bend.

"This is it, but I think we can go in from the other side."

He has slowed and turned off, passing a filthy old Volvo and an equally beat-up Chevy van with tie-dye curtains across the windows. Behind the barricade of these vehicles, I glimpse a skinny man of unknowable age silhouetted in tatters, a wild frizz of ponytail and bits of escaped hair with a supersized bottle of beer. I am suddenly very happy to be "going in from the other side."

We soon discover a wide, barbed-wire gate blocking the path we were hoping to take. It is posted with "keep out" and "no trespassing" signs, so we walk back to the van and station wagon parked in front of the main trail entrance. Peering around the vehicles, we see another wide gate with "keep out" signs. Standing with the tattered frizz man, a smaller blonde man releases a volume of smoke coloring the eucalyptus air.

"When did they close this off?"

"S'been a while." A yellow-toothed grimace. "They don't want no one in there."

"I've been there. It's a beautiful spot. Just getting too trampled?"

"Yeah, man, just 'magine that you're only one of the ten thousands of people that come here thinkin' it's their spot. Their secret spot." Spoken with another pungent release of smoke that swirls all around his head and body, mixing to a golden haze in the dust and sunlight and the curl of his lips on the word "secret."

"Yeah, well, it's a beautiful spot." Wistful, he turns to me, turns to the gate, and takes my hand. "Take care."

We start back to the car.

"That's a shock."

"I don't even know how to feel—how to think about that. It's a big shock." He sounds shaken.

Does he feel as if you have again been ripped out of his life?

I stay quiet. Do I console or give him the space to know his feelings? Although I have wondered what to expect in the moments when the three of us would come together in this place, there are different questions now. I have a sense of irony—that death has its final word yet again, denying the resolution he surely intended as he embraces our new life side by side with his old one.

Over the next hours we talk about the irony, the shock of those closed gates and forbidden access—of what it all means. I see that he is letting it roll around in his brain along with the sadness of the day and whatever unmet expectation he might feel. Over dinner, we chat with an affable waiter about wines and Santa Barbara, living at home after graduating, and plans for medical school. We circle the shock as if by sampling every dimension of our feelings, we will find understanding.

"I still don't know how to think about it."

"It feels so ironic to me."

"It's a message of some sort."

"Message?"

"It couldn't have been more clear that access was blocked off—denied." Seconds later he adds. "I kind of wanted to say, 'When did you get so private?' "

"You must feel disappointed."

"It's not that. I'm not disappointed. I've been ready to let go. I want to understand."

His processing peppers our conversation between stories of their life together and stories shared as our waiter brings dishes and then clears them. I wonder if we will make love, or if the day truly belongs to his memories and the Ventana wilderness. He orders apple pie made famous by the owners of the inn and is quickly served a large slice with a mound of vanilla ice cream. We make plans to hike, visit coastal art galleries, and buy fresh crab the next day. We return to our room and make love with urgency that we both understand.

In the morning, we step outside to soft breezes and sun filtering through the redwoods. Crossing the road he says, "Let's go to the river after we eat."

Again in the rustic dining room, we linger over oatmeal and coffee.

"What a day yesterday, certainly not what we came here for or expected…" I say. "Do you want to…."

"No, I've been ready—I don't want to go back." He sits up very straight. "That time is over and done. The message could not be more clear—it's time for us, time to go on, our time."

In the Wings of a Wedding

Stars with lighted points and glowing centers hang from white peaks that canopy the courtyard where we are to be married. From where I stand, tucked away from the 150 or so guests, I miss the entrance of the officiant, groomsmen and groom. I am re-positioned close enough to hear the collective intake of breath as two statuesque bridesmaids, my daughters, walk themselves down the aisle. There are murmurs as the three and a half year-old flower girl enters in a full-length black tutu and ribboned wreath, carrying her basket of bright petals. Chuckles come next as our ring bearer, a five-year-old in a straw fedora, makes his way from the rear to his parents in the front row. The wedding has begun.

We are not young things. We are neither groping toward adulthood nor cocky in our precociousness. This is not our first marriage. In fact, we would still be happily married to spouses we loved dearly, if not for the ravages dealt them by cancer. We did not, in the beginning, look at each other with anything other than professional interest and respect. We had known each other in the community for a decade, serving in nonprofits. That all changed—maybe over months, maybe in a conversation, in a day, and then in minutes.

It sealed itself at a collegial dinner when Michael sat close and moved ever closer to me. A friend later said, "He's a little pushy."

He walked me to my car and gave me a long, but flat, stage kiss. When he called the next day, I wondered aloud, "What is your real kiss like?"

That moment was the beginning of long hours at my kitchen island, dinnertime music-surfing his 17,000-plus iTunes songs, in conversations that sent us to Siri to research the Bay of Pigs, the life of Rhassan Roland Kirk and the hospital at the University of Chicago where we were both born—albeit many years ago and three and a half years apart.

Falling in love was not the prolonged intake of breath that it had been as a younger person. Love at this stage of life, so unexpected, felt both wonderful and, for both of us, like a betrayal of the spouses we had loved for many years—and still did these years after their passing.

Eight months after Michael moved in, his wedding candle from Melinda remained on the kitchen island for weeks. Was it a shrine, a holding on, an expression of conflict, a thought in process?

I wondered as he moved it from the counter to the trunk of his car before it disappeared. Much later he told me he threw it out. "It was just a thing."

For my part, I rationalized pictures of my late husband throughout the house with the idea that this was my daughters' family home, and it would be another loss for them to find their father removed. Gradually, old photos did disappear from the credenzas, shelves and incidental tables they once occupied.

What came with falling in love again was a rush of memory and resistance. Why did we need to rearrange the couch and chairs in the family room, sit in different places at the dining room table, and turn the bedroom that once housed a daughter into a sitting room/office?

Grief is like that. It wants to hold you and you want to hold it because it seems to keep you close to the person who is gone.

So, we balanced falling in love with the love we would always feel for the spouses we had lost. They were with us as surely as if they were by our side in each room of the house.

The changes as we merged households again affirmed the ones of the six years that had passed. Knowing in my heart that I wanted Michael at my side for the rest of my days, over a period of weeks, I became sanguine with the mix of elation, upset, and joy.

As important was the happiness with which both girls embraced Michael. "He's fantastic, Mom," whispered the twenty-one-year-old shortly after meeting him for the first time. The kitchen became a demonstration site for Aikido principles of circularity, which Michael taught both girls, and a cross-generational sharing of music from Matisyahu, the rabbi rapper, to Pink Martini and Rupa and the April Fishes.

Michael and I carved out time from our work lives to drive to Port Townsend, move the youngest girl to school at UCLA, and move her older sister from her Berkeley apartment to San Francisco. He officiated his goddaughter's wedding in LA after which we packaged and shipped our dressy clothes home, taking a single bag across country to the pastel-and-deco shine of Florida's South Beach. We spent a few days meeting family of our late spouses and then joined a small group on a charter flight bound for Havana.

Our trips were about ferns that grew from the walls of a narrow canyon near the Oregon border, shiny-faced kids he'd loved all their lives, in-laws who shared everything but my DNA, cobblestone streets that contained no sewer or water systems, oppressed people with irrepressible expression in music, painting, dance, smiles—the beating heart declaring its freedom.

We had another haven, my mountain cabin on the shore of a tiny Sierra lake. We traveled there early in our days of discovering each other and returned for the New Year where Michael proposed on bent knee. Home again, we walked around the house with a single art object, convinced that the art we brought to our new life "declared" its chosen display space. We shifted more furniture and built a man cave, "the shed."

With all this as our foundation, we entered the weekend leading to our wedding— the days we had designated to gather friends, our families, and the families of our late spouses in celebration of our union. We knew it would be bittersweet.

The night before the wedding began in a balconied room with unromantic lighting, less-than-gourmet hors d'oeuvres, and springless vintage couches and chairs— the loft of a downtown jazz club. Four families had come together, some meeting for the first time. Some had come to terms with our marriage; others held firm to the idea that the new spouse would be an inferior stand-in for the one who was gone. In a corner, positioned against the club's red-brick wall, sax and guitar musicians served up jazz standards that got the occasional couple dancing, but most of the time remained background for chatter.

Our Italian friends burst into the room, breathless with excitement about the band setting up to play downstairs later in the evening.

"It is so incredible! This group will play the Stratus tonight."

The Stratus keyboard synthesizer featured signal processing chips designed by my late husband, an instrument he designed in collaboration with our daughter's Italian godfather. Ashley got doe-eyed and tearful.

Through the evening, a young server circled the room, taking drink orders. With long dark hair pulled back into a high ponytail, and a litheness and fluidity of movement, she had the appearance of a dancer. Someone asked, making reference to the many people in the room who were involved with local arts organizations.

"No, I don't dance but my mom did. She worked with a choreographer named…."

And there it was, Michael's late wife had worked with the server's mother.

A day later, I enter the stucco arch where I am cued to start my walk. The audience stands. One-two-three-four-five, I count to myself, looking briefly at people I recognize on each side of the aisle. There are some I only recently met, friends of the man I am marrying, and some who have been friends for decades. Many, like the Italians, who catch my eye, have traveled to join in this celebration. Looking at each of my girls flanking the spot where we will speak our vows, I set my gaze straight ahead on my beaming groom.

All Becomes New

Ashley and Nima wed under a tall stand of redwoods in 2016. Julia agonized until the last minute, then sang a cappella to be joined by voices from the audience who stood, one, then another and then a fourth.

Now I had a married daughter, a son-in-law, Nima. A whole group of Persian families on Nima's side attended. Most, like his own, did not speak English. I had learned something about their shared religion, Baha'i and tried to honor their culture and religion with readings in Farsi, as well as our English ones. We served steak, pasta and chicken catered by a local Iranian-owned restaurant. The owner carefully infused saffron, pomegranate and other cultural flavors.

We had met up with Ashley and Nima in Italy in 2015 and traveled to see Ashley's godfather, Rossano, at his beach house in Numana. I remember the town as a stop after Doug's busy work days when Rossano pulled the car to a sleepy place near a modest, stone building. He'd say in Italian, "Here's what they have today, of course fresh caught. Please, please help yourself." The meal was always beyond expectation.

That memory of thirty-five years ago (maybe more) featured fresh "fruits of the sea" laid out buffet-style where we sampled every one onto our plates. Now with Ashley and Nima we dined at the same restaurant enlarged into a busy sprawl, tables of six and more diners, tables overflowing with shellfish, crab legs, clams, sauteed white fish and, of course, the obligatory bowls of pasta.

After seeing Rossano and sharing a night of cacio e pepe, we traveled separately and met up again in Rome. We knew that Nima had driven around for months with an engagement ring of his own design in the trunk of his car. He had consulted with Julia and me, choosing a setting that closely resembled the twenty-five-year ring that Doug gave me nine days before his passing. But the diamond in Nima's engagement ring was circled in a pink display, very Ashley. It felt like this was the time to deliver that ring.

The morning after arriving, we answered a call. "Meet us at the top of the Spanish Steps." Nima and Ashley approached us. She held up her gleaming diamond as Nima smiled wide.

In the years after losing Doug, I had rebuilt the guest house after a catastrophic burst pipe, planted a small orchard, remodeled our kitchen while completing my MFA, and made plans for new floors in the hall and master bedroom. I signed the contract a week or two after Michael moved in. The clothes he had placed in neat order had to be removed to the living room as did racks of clothes from the closet. We plopped our king-sized mattress onto the rug in what was once Ashley's room and slept there for two weeks while oak planks replaced tired carpet in the hall and master bedroom. My life seemed to renew on a regular timetable. At times I railed against change.

Why did the couch in the family room have to swap sides with the chairs? Did we really need a bigger screen? Did the living room couch really need to be moved? And yet I embraced it all. All that I knew transformed into a new life taking me with it.

Three years after meeting the kids on the Spanish Steps, we were awakened before dawn by an call.

"I'm taking Ashley to the hospital."

It was 6 a.m. Though she was sent home, Nima's call triggered mine to Julia, who jumped on the first plane to San Francisco.

Another call as we pulled out of SFO with Julia in the back seat. "We're going back, Mom. I came home and made pancakes and the pain got bad."

Our cars met on the Potrero hillside where, as we traveled up, we met Nima driving down to UCSF Benioff Hospital. This time they kept Ashley. It was the real thing.

"Ashley, I'll be wherever you need me to be, in or out of the delivery room." I thought about those words before saying them. Having had both girls by C-section, all I really knew firsthand about delivery was my own hard labor with Ashley (followed by an emergency C-section) and what I heard when touring a client's gleaming new hospital, then hearing the screams of a woman pushing her baby out in a nearby, closed room. Knowing that every delivery is as different as the woman and the family, I would take my cues from Ashley.

At first we congregated in the waiting room with an Oculus experience for diversion, thanks to her close friend who works in that division of Google. Somehow we got word that we were invited in, one by one, and then Julia and I were just there with Ashley and Nima, witnessing her restless quiet, her agonized movement around the room, her hand on her back as intense pain seized her in cycles. A woman in labor, my daughter.

I was honored that she wanted us there. We were there for the big decision after a midwife came in and said, "Honey, you're here to have a baby, not to be in pain. It's time to have an epidural and some Pitocin, so you can sleep and then push that baby out!"

Ashley had been determined to have the baby naturally, but after eighteen hours of hard labor, she was exhausted. I happily supported the advice. It was 1 a.m., and we left for some sleep at our SF condo.

At 5 a.m. we woke to Nima's text. "Kai waltzed into this world at 4:55."

Our family photos introduce Kai Aiden Rad, a not-so-tiny boy, born twenty-one inches long to his tall parents. Julia sobbed with a smile, seeing him for the first time.

Across many cultures, Kai has meanings of ocean or sea; his middle name is fiery one from Celtic origins. In the Persian tradition, Aiden is "enlightened one."

Blue eyes and reddish-blonde hair have asserted Ashley's heritage, despite his dad's genes. He laughed in his sleep as a tiny infant—many times. I would gaze at him in my arms, studying his long, blonde eyelashes, wispy strawberry-blonde hair, long fingers, and steady soft breathing, my mind dreamy in wakefulness as his was at rest. In this tiny being, new life presented to us, and we stepped into each moment with new intention. I knew that all of us would teach him about the stars and the constellations, the ways of the animals, the differences in the cultures of people and the ways in which they live. I knew he would have questions about so much and answers would come with stories of great tribes and empires, gods, goddesses, warriors, and peacemakers. From his first day, he responded to sound and music. I remembered that could very likely foreshadow an ability with math and the sciences. As much as he might inherit all of that from his parents and extended family, I knew he would quickly show us a different person, his own unique self, separate and distinct from all of us. I made a vow to know him well, to truly be his Mimi Joon.

I told Ashley, "I don't just want to be a grandmother, I want to be IN his life."

Although Ashley and Julia had always refused to travel anywhere for Christmas, I seized on the newness of this time to offer a family Christmas in Hawaii. Both girls liked the idea. Nima did too.

Airline miles got us seats in first class where we boarded and were met by withering stares of our other privileged cabinmates. Baby Kai fussed at first, sucked with vigor on a small bottle during takeoff, and settled to quiet in oversized, blue, noise- cancelling headphones during the flight. Another vigorous suck on a bottle grounded us in Kona.

This was a new sort of honeymoon. We all had fallen love with a very tiny, life- changing new family member.

The Big Island greeted us with humidity, an open-air airport, and the confusion of finding our way to our rented Jeep and bigger SUV. We caravaned the coastal road to a turn uphill and a twisty road up to a turn and another after passing goats and a pig pasturing at one side of the road. Down a rutted driveway and there we were, our home for a week.

In this comfortable house, complete with lighted Christmas tree, we lived like family, cooking, taking turns caring for our newest one. He napped in a cushioned, portable bed on the coffee table. We rushed to his cry.

Somehow, I had him in my arms in the crying time before morning naps. I found a large mirror and distracted him.

"Kai, fuusssy baaby! Look Kai, look at the fussy baby!" I said it in a singing voice, and it seemed that the song captured his attention.

Of course, it was almost a year too early for him to recognize anything but an image in the mirror. As that image exhausted him, I gathered him into my arms where he fell asleep on my shoulder, soon to be lowered onto his cushioned coffee-table dock.

When we emerged from our cocoon house, Kai was a movie star in lime-green rimmed, blue-lensed glasses, his nearly bald head protected from the sun by blue hat, his portochair or the cabana we purchased poolside one day. Ashley, ever the swim instructor from her country club job in college days, brought Kai to the swimming pool, floating him and even splashing water on his head and face. He seemed to like the gentle, new sensations. Nima, not a sand or water person, enjoyed the cabana for a good long time before joining his family.

Yellow lizards imprinted their curiousity outside our pebbled bathroom windows at the house. Enveloped gifts adorned the branches of the living room tree. Christmas Eve we all dressed in our one nice outfit for a more formal dinner at the Fairmont Orchid, but aside from that, we shopped local grocery stores and cooked fresh fish in our "home." Julia posed for me atop a flat, lava rock and again for her own phone, smiling in profile against stormy waves. Palm trees at angles stilled before weather tilted them into a wind. We stopped on the lush farm of a friend from my MFA cohort, touring the pasture, pausing to scratch the ears of Nubian goats who gazed at us with slit-pupiled eyes. We toured the island's perimeter one rainy day and made the trip up Mauna Kea, billed on signage as an Ice Age preserve. The terrain darkened with increasing lava composition, the temperature dropped and somewhere before 9,000 feet Kai cried, striking out with his little limbs. He quieted when we reversed our course down the altitude; we knew again we listened to a new voice, one that would be with us as a glorious addition to our family.

It was a time of crimson sunsets, double rainbows against a slate sky, abundant trumpet flowerings, tropical churches set low under royal skies, cemetery crosses celebrated by gardenia and jasmine in jungle-rich bushes. A nighttime snorkel turned up a group of rays. In town, Banyan trees stretched over coastal thoroughfares as folks in bright clothing clustered in chatter beneath.

All I knew gentled over time into this new life. I counted on my genes to keep me in the lives of Kai and other grandchildren who I planned on and planned to know well. What comes to me now after seeing the ceremony of tribal crossings in San Juan de Fuca, from the desire to preserve tradition: something very different.

To Kai and all my grandchildren, we come from ancient roots and mysteries of heredity that we cannot know, marked only in trinkets and faded photos. You are more than the yellowed old squares and the charm bracelet from a Nonni you never knew. You will never know Doug, your grandpa. You have cousins to meet. A new world opens with you and for you. You rise on the shoulders of all your forbears. You are the first with the great burden. You are the worthy ones given by destiny to lead our families into the sunlight, whimsy, and scrutiny that you grab in your hold.

I am now the ancestor from our side, and before going on with my joyous new life, I added these words as a preface to my will.

Before you read the text in the sections below, I want to share a little about Douglas Reid Curtis, who you will unfortunately never have the chance to know. You may have heard stories about him as your grandfather, or perhaps he was your great grandfather.

A self-made man by virtue of being willing to study anything in depth, he was a quiet and brilliant inventor, an entrepreneur, an athelete and adventurer, a man with a warm heart for his friends and devotion to his family, and a resolutely independent thinker who above all else lived by the creed "do the right thing."

In 2006, as he suffered the ravages of pancreatic cancer, he and I sat down to author guidance for our heirs which I now pass on to you as a set of family principles.

What do we wish for you above all else? We wish that you and your descendants find happiness and joy in every day by living a balanced and principled life.

As you make your way through what you will read next, pause for a moment to reflect on this. We address you here with great love, joy, and pride and all that we accomplish together.

Meditation on a Fallen Tree

A loud and sudden *whoosh* alerted me first. I turned to see the live oak tree swaying violently outside my window, as if an earthquake or a gale force wind had swept through its branches and shaken every leaf. In the middle of the long house where I sat, the ground had not moved. Next, the sound of my husband calling my name in a voice that sounded small, shaken.

"Did you hear it? Do you know what that was?"

"It seemed like there was a strong gust of wind," I ventured.

"It was the sound of the big oak tree falling."

We moved to the front door and outside. Before us, where seven trunks had majestically reached to the sky…nothing. Peering downhill over the front porch rail, I saw the great thing sprawled across the tiny orchard, footpath, driveway and third terrace of hillside below, a giant felled. Broken, now in thick chaos, it had ripped apart smaller trees on its fall, having torn clean somewhere below the soil. A deep gash opened in the dirt where it once anchored. An empty twilight sky yawned where a lace of trunks and leaves once offered shelter. What happened to the creatures who took refuge in its crannies? And what arteries and perches would serve the crows, the squirrels, chickadees and finches, woodpeckers and ring-necked doves? In my forty years living here, this grand Valley Oak greeted all who came to this place, the heart and soul of this estate. And the creatures who came to its branches—spirit messengers—commanded our attention through the full-height picture windows of the house we had built.

Many times over many years, I repeated to myself how beautiful this tree, what a fortunate landmark nature had placed for us. Reverential and filled with gratitude, I felt as if this tree were part of our family. I addressed thoughts of admiration to the tree like a lover would honor each day with a love, admiring the tree's statuesque beauty as I passed it in the driveway. To me this glorious oak was a standing landmark of the property hundreds of years before it was built with any homes, perhaps a shelter to the Muwekma Ohlone tribe that predated our town and our family. Perhaps they chose one of its trunks to scale as a lookout or a vantage point on the big cats, turkeys, coyotes, raccoons, skunks and quail that attempt a coexistence on these hillsides. Our oak welcomed and embraced all who arrived, rose as the great protector of all life here, a guardian of my life after Doug passed. This great Valley Oak lifted me again and again with its seven trunks, its branches for sassy crows, stops for voracious woodpeckers, springing squirrels, doves and many other unseen creatures of a tree.

I barely understood the cascade of emotions starting in me as feeble harbingers of the grieving the next days would bring.

"Oh my God, oh my God." I must have said the words from every angle where I surveyed the sad scene.

It was cold. I could not bring myself to get close to it. I had to talk to the girls who had grown up under the lush canopy of this patriarch. They wept with me, seeing the carnage on their phones from where I stood behind living room windows.

We told ourselves that it was so lucky the tree fell in that direction, sparing the guest house to the right where Michael worked out, and our home to its left where I sat at a desk - humans in either direction where it could have toppled. But that was logic and common sense. The deeper sense pointed to no logic, only loss again. I asked myself what this meant. What did this portend? All I could point to —the tangle of branches, the crushed orchard fencing and fruit trees, the blackened tree base, an irregular shape that reached a six-foot diameter in places, and the gash in the soil.

We were no strangers to loss. I remembered the years after my Doug's death, the many times I caught myself instinctively turning to where he sat to ask a question that needed his answer. But he was gone then, his favorite leather chair without him, cold and empty. The girls continued their march to adulthood, marking graduations, travels and future times when he would not be there. Before she married, the oldest debated long and hard about who would walk her down the aisle, resolving finally on her godfather and her new step-dad, Michael. The youngest settled quickly, saying I would walk her down the aisle when she marries. She measures the years that he's been gone against her own. With this year's birthday, she will have spent half her life without her dad.

Seven years ago, I married Michael, who also knew loss. Once happily married like me, he knew the ravages of a cancer that took his wife. Later in the night the Valley Oak fell, he would simply say, "I feel like I'm grieving."

As much as there was so much to be done, nothing—no act or thought—could undo this loss, no consolation or remedy, only the fact. A count and calculation of its rings aged the tree at 262 years. An ancient spirit, a treasure, another living one we loved had been torn from our soils and our hearts.

Yes, the gardener came and will begin clearing on Monday. Insurance will return my call. We will rebuild fences and plant new fruit trees. We will even plant a new tree, that at fifteen feet, will look like a puny sapling in the spot that the oak commanded. The new tree's roots are needed to hold the hill that slopes downward to the tree, its branches offering new arteries, perches and nooks for all that live on this property. I will take photos from every angle to document material loss. Both life and loss go on. But that's all logic and common sense. Moving forward cannot fill the gash, color the void or erase our sadness. It merely affirms that we remain alive.

The falling of this tree does portend a finite existence, ours. Michael and I are healthy, but, like the highway fatality as we drove to San Francisco Monday, we are all subject to wild fate. The tree had rotted at the roots. A tiny car driver collided with a truck. Both ends, sudden and unpredictable.

The great Valley Oak, a family member like so many of our own who have lived to an old age for our species, instills our resolve to live long and fall with grace.

Mary Pacifico Curtis is a Silicon Valley entrepreneur, seasoned branding and PR professional, and author of poetry and non-fiction. Published work includes two poetry chapbooks, Between Rooms and The White Tree Quartet (WordTech's Turning Point imprint), and numerous pickups in literary magazines and anthologies. Accolades include recognition as a 2012 Joy Harjo Poetry Finalist (Cutthroat Journal), 2019 Poetry Finalist in The Tiferet Journal, non-fiction finalist in The 48th New Millenium Writings contest and a 2021 non-fiction finalist in The Tupelo Quarterly Open.

At 24, she founded Pacifico, Inc., which grew into one of Silicon Valley's largest independently owned PR and branding firms with clients that included many global technology leaders.

When both daughters went off to college, she earned an MFA in 2012 in creative writing from Goddard College.

Curtis lives with her husband in the foothills of the Santa Cruz mountains on a terraced property where she grows vegetables and fends off gophers while admiring deer, coyotes, wild turkeys and the occasional bobcat.

30127351R00078